STRESS IS RELATIVE!

A Woman's Take on Air Traffic Control

Memoir

By Rose Marie Kern

Stress is Relative!

Stress is Relative!
A Woman's Take on Air Traffic Control
All Rights Reserved.
Copyright ©March 2018 Rose Marie Kern
www.rosemariekern.com

Warning and Disclaimer
Every effort has been made to make this book as complete and as accurate as possible, but no warranty or fitness is implied. The information provided is on an "as is" basis. The author and the publisher shall have neither liability nor responsibility to any person or entity with respect to any loss or damages arising from the information contain in this book.

This is a memoir; therefore the events and circumstances of this memoir are real, but subject to one person's perspectives. Most of the names have been changed. Conversations are not verbatim; they were re-created to the best of the author's ability.

For information about buying this title in bulk quantities or for special sales opportunities (which may include electronic versions) please contact our corporate sales department at solarranch@swcp.com

This book may not be reproduced, transmitted, or stored in whole or in part by any means, including graphic, electronic or mechanical without the express written consent of the author except in the case of brief quotations embodied in critical articles and reviews.

Solar Ranch Publishing   1655 Flora Vista DR. SW   Albuquerque, NM 87105

ISBN-13: 978-0-9985725-1-2
Library of Congress control number   1-6268667351

Stress is Relative!

Dedicated to
Vitus Francis and Marie Huser Kern

My loving parents, who encouraged all their
children to follow their dreams.

Stress is Relative!

Acknowledgements

One thing I have learned as a writer is that in order to produce the best possible article or book, you must put it first into the hands of those who understand what you are doing and have the knowledge, skills and abilities to help you made it the best it can be.

I want to thank these people from my heart for their time and expertise:

Melissa Dawson

Carolyn Dawson

Sarah Rowe

Steve Prout

Dollie Williams

Some of my friends are very talented photographers. Though most of the pictures herein are my own, I want to thank the following people for enhancing the book with photos they gave me permission to use.

Dennis Livesay

Jeff Shephard

Scott Cunningham

Stress is Relative!

FORWARD

It's funny how you can be disassociated emotionally as you look back over 34 years of working within the Air Traffic Control arena. The perspective changes when you see all the good and bad things at a distance and realize that if each little step had not been taken you would be a different person.

Leaving Indiana in 1983 I was the stereotype of, as my husband says, "A good little Catholic girl." For the most part I did what was expected of me, never cussed, never bucked authority, and could be intimidated fairly easily.

A loving childhood, and a voracious appetite for reading, leads to many successes in academics and in my initial work environments. The harsh criticisms endured during ATC training took some getting used to. I like to think of the FAA Academy as an advanced assertiveness training school.

I learned to stand my ground when male counterparts tried to either force me out of the job or seduce me, and though I am not a vindictive person, I am now confident enough and knowledgeable enough about the system to know when I should and can resort to legal measures to defend myself.

With the blind luck of youth, I stumbled into a career that I had never dreamed existed. Though the first years were challenging, eventually I excelled to the point that I was awarded three national and four regional awards during my career.

I encountered both the best and worst of men and women in this line of work. The worst ones would undercut or try to diminish anyone who was different then themselves. The best of them saw the potential every person possesses and offered support, friendship and a smile.

The job forced me to move to a place that I quickly learned to love and today I enjoy a great relationship with the flying community. I write monthly columns on various aspects of ATC and aviation weather in seven aviation publications and have had individual articles published in others. Many pilots have asked for a book that would combine the knowledge of those articles into one place – so I wrote a compilation entitled "Air to Ground".

Because so few women even know that ATC exists as a career choice, I wanted to showcase the steps I took to get into this highly lucrative field. In many ways, especially since the government has been proactive in creating and monitoring equal opportunity and sexual harassment regulations, it is an ideal job for women because it requires intelligence and quick decision making.

Many times over the years I've thought that executive secretaries, scout leaders, or mothers of large families would make good Air Traffic controllers because they are used to keeping track of and directing the movements of groups of people all going different directions. ATC requires that skill along with practical knowledge of how computers function and a good general learning aptitude.

One of the most important elements a woman needs is a good sense of self, an inner strength and the ability to weather the challenges and disappointments as well as the successes of the job.

This memoir begins during an interesting time in history. A U.S. President who had previously been the President of a union, fired all members of the Professional Air Traffic Controllers Organization union (PATCO) who were on strike, more than 11,000 people. It took years to rebuild the system.

Most of the general public does not know that there was (and is) a no-strike clause in the employment contract for controllers – yet

PATCO had orchestrated several "sick outs" and slow-downs prior to the infamous strike. Each time it happened, the air traffic system was dramatically disrupted; this one was the last straw.

Although the Civil Rights Act of 1964 prohibits employment discrimination based on race, color, religion, sex, or national origin, implementing that ideal, even in government jobs, took decades, and is still ongoing. In 1983, two years after the strike, the concept of equality was an ideal facing opposition in professions historically dominated by males. The Air Traffic Control workforce was 94% Caucasian males, the majority of which had come from military backgrounds.

Training was supposed to be standardized, but outside of those tests that were on paper, all actions relating to job performance were scored subject to the trainer's personal standards and opinions in combination with the requirements dictated by the FAA Operational Orders.

This book begins before I went to the Academy and primarily follows my career progression, the challenges I faced, the decisions I made, and the moves I made between facilities. It continues along my career pathway until retirement. Along the way it explains a little more about how Air Traffic Control functions as I relate my own discoveries.

The world's view of women's roles changed a great deal during this era. Government regulations concerning Equal Employment were disliked by many, which complicated an already difficult career path and yet eventually led to a more balanced environment.

Stress is Relative!

Ronald Reagan

40th President of the United States of America

Stress is Relative!

Speech made by President Ronald Reagan to Reporters on the Air Traffic Controller's Strike

August 3, 1981 10:55 a.m. in the Rose Garden at the White House

"This morning at 7 a.m. the union representing those who man America's air traffic control facilities called a strike. This was the culmination of 7 months of negotiations between the Federal Aviation Administration and the union. At one point in these negotiations agreement was reached and signed by both sides, granting a $40 million increase in salaries and benefits. This is twice what other government employees can expect. It was granted in recognition of the difficulties inherent in the work these people perform. Now, however, the union demands are 17 times what had been agreed to -- $681 million. This would impose a tax burden on their fellow citizens which is unacceptable.

I would like to thank the supervisors and controllers who are on the job today, helping to get the nation's air system operating safely. In the New York area, for example, four supervisors were scheduled to report for work, and 17 additionally volunteered. At National Airport a traffic controller told a newsperson he had resigned from the union and reported to work because, ``How can I ask my kids to obey the law if I don't?'' This is a great tribute to America.

Stress is Relative!

Let me make one thing plain. I respect the right of workers in the private sector to strike. Indeed, as president of my own union, I led the first strike ever called by that union. I guess I'm maybe the first one to ever hold this office who is a lifetime member of an AFL - CIO union. But we cannot compare labor-management relations in the private sector with government.
Government cannot close down the assembly line. It has to provide without interruption the protective services which are government's reason for being.

It was in recognition of this that the Congress passed a law forbidding strikes by government employees against the public safety. Let me read the solemn oath taken by each of these employees, a sworn affidavit, when they accepted their jobs: `I am not participating in any strike against the Government of the United States or any agency thereof, and I will not so participate while an employee of the Government of the United States or any agency thereof.'

It is for this reason that I must tell those who fail to report for duty this morning they are in violation of the law, and if they do not report for work within 48 hours, they have forfeited their jobs and will be terminated."

CHAPTER 1

Discovering an Opportunity

I don't tend to watch the evening news very often, but for some reason there I was, sitting on the couch after dinner listening to CBS. It was August 3, 1982 – one year after President Reagan fired 80% of the nation's air traffic controllers.

The reporter was interviewing ex-Air Traffic Control union guys who kept talking about how the strike was called because Controllers deserved to get higher salaries because of the amount of stress the job forced on them, because they had to work odd hours, and a host of other complaints that at the time frankly seemed like whining.

After all, there are a lot of jobs where people have to work odd hours under stressful conditions – just ask police and firefighters!

When the TV showed a salary chart my eyebrows lifted. It was 10 times as much as I was making!

Then they spoke to a government official who told the viewers that they were still hiring replacements and would be for some time to come.

At that point in time I was working essentially two jobs and trying to raise my daughters on my own. It was tough – I needed to be able to maintain a secure home in a safe neighborhood. The girls were still very young and I had been hoping for a promotion or a pathway to a new higher paying job.

Stress is Relative!

Something in the back of my mind kept thinking about that news report. I kept going over it and analyzing my current situation.

I was 27 years old, in good health with shoulder length red hair and blue eyes. Monday through Friday I worked as an assistant in the International division of Merchants Bank. In the evenings and on weekends I taught children's theater and took contract work to direct plays, or do other backstage work at local theaters.

At least my kids could go with me to the theaters and they really enjoyed being backstage. Several times the Indianapolis Opera Company had a need for small children, so my daughters performed onstage for *Il Trovatore* and *The Magic Flute*.

Even with the two jobs I was constantly trying to save money – lots of cheesy tuna and noodles or hot dog dinners, eating at my parents' house occasionally, riding the bus instead of wasting automobile gas.

A need to be as good a parent as possible drove me to working two jobs and left no time to finish my degree in Arts Administration, which I had hoped would lead to a good solid well-paying job. How was I going to be able to keep my daughters in a safe environment and become the kind of role model that they could look up to?

So, as you can see, STRESS is relative.

The world of ATC would be very different from offices and theater…but a nagging interest inspired by the news report prompted me to call the Federal Office of Personnel Management the next morning. It felt really stupid, but I asked the OPM representative "How do you become an Air Traffic Controller?"

Her answer surprised me. "You take a test."

A TEST? A TEST! I am REALLY good at tests. Don't ask me why but I have always had a knack for tests…especially those multiple choice things. After all, without any work at all you have a one in four chance of passing.

Stress is Relative!

If I passed the test, the Federal Aviation Administration (FAA) would not only give me all the training I needed, but pay me almost twice what I was making now while doing so.

The OPM representative told me the next test would take place in about a month and took my name. A week later the preliminary forms and a test registration arrived in the mail. The test would only be the first step, but it was necessary to pass it before you were eligible for anything else.

If I knew that the challenges I would be facing were more than just learning the job I might have stopped right there, but at that point in my life I had excelled at anything academic and I really had no idea what I was getting into. Like most average people I had seen tall slender towers in movies and at Indianapolis International airport, and the cinema occasionally showed a radar. How all of it fit together or what the job entailed was a complete mystery, but I figured, "What the heck".

Like the "Fool" card in a Tarot deck, I was about to step off the ledge of a mountain not knowing what was ahead of me, but knowing that if I did not take a step in some direction, nothing would change.

My boss approved leave on the day of the test, though I did not indicate the reason I wanted off. Heck, regardless of past successes there was only a slim chance I would ever pass this unknown test anyway – I knew ZERO about airplanes or airports.

Lesson Learned – Don't limit the vision of your future to what people expect of you.

Stress is Relative!

CHAPTER 2

The Air Traffic Control Exam

On the day of the ATC test I took the bus into downtown Indianapolis as usual, but instead of getting off a block from the bank where I worked, I exited by the federal building.

Like most government buildings the architect strove to create something that projected a feeling of solidity and permanence. There were high ceilings, tall marble columns and that slightly musty smell of old buildings. It looked like about fifty people were waiting outside the doors of the room where the test was given.

And the variety of people! I expected to see people in generally standard office dress, but that was just the beginning. There were guys in overalls, jeans and tee shirts, others looked almost homeless – unwashed, unshaven, messy hair. A few were dressed up as though they were going to an interview with shiny shoes and briefcases.

The vast majority of hopeful candidates were male,. I only saw a couple women standing outside the doors. Little was I to know that this was the way it would always be in ATC. It just wasn't a profession parents brought up as a possibility to their daughters. You didn't see any "Air Traffic Controller" or "Pilot" Barbie dolls growing up.

The doors opened. The crowd in the foyer surged in and took seats at tables already set with test forms and pencils. We answered to a roll call. The test monitor told us there would be a total of seven tests. Four

Stress is Relative!

of the tests were based on scenarios, the next two were IQ tests, and the last one was a test of our knowledge of aviation. The interesting part was that the last test would not count in our overall grade, but it did give up to five extra points if we did well.

All of them were timed, multiple choice questions. The first four started simply but got progressively more complicated. There were diagrams representing airways...kind of like streets in the sky. These airways intersected and where they crossed or ended was a letter. In places on the airways were dots representing airplanes with identifications next to them.

Next to the diagram were lists showing the aircraft identification, and letters corresponding to the ones on the chart were grouped to show what route the aircraft would fly, their airspeed and their altitudes.

The rules were fairly simple. The aircraft had to stay separated from each other by either altitude or distance: they had to be either 1000 feet above or below the other aircraft, or 5 miles apart. The altitude was easy to see, the distance and closure rates had to be calculated based on the airspeed and the distance measurement line.

Each test had 50 questions all of which were a variation on "Which two aircraft will come into conflict?" The first set had an easy diagram with only three or four aircraft. The diagrams became more complex with each test, and contained up to 16 aircraft in the last one. You had 35 minutes to complete each test – under a minute per question.

It was fun.

* * * * *

To my knowledge a variety of this test is still being administered to ATC applicants, so I will digress a moment with a description.

Stress is Relative!

Aircraft	Altitude	Airspeed	Routing
N121PA	5000	120 knots	A-J-H-D
R22456	6000	120 knots	C-G-J-F
N3RJ	6000	240 knots	C-G-J-A
UAL1022	7000	240 knots	B-G-H-D
N34567	3000	120 knots	A-J-H-D
DLA101	8000	240 knots	D-H-J-A

SCALE |---------| = 10 MILES

Which two aircraft could come into conflict?

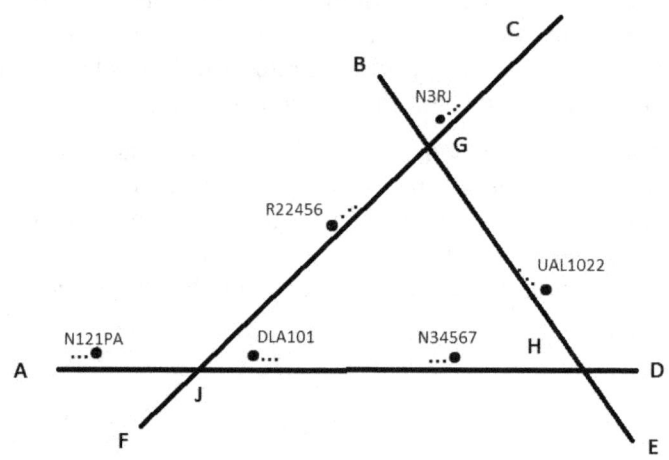

Stress is Relative!

In the example shown there are only two aircraft which could come into conflict. Each aircraft is represented by a big dot with three little dots "trailing behind". All but two are already separated by altitude. N3RJ is behind R22456 traveling the same direction, but N3RJ is doing 240 Knots speed – approximately 4 miles a minute. R22456 is only doing 120 knots – 2 miles a minute. The scale shows them approximately 20 miles apart – so within 10 minutes N3RJ could overtake R22456.

I always liked logic puzzles, mysteries, lost item scenarios, etc... This was the culmination. It went on to be even better with the IQ portions. The first IQ portion was numbers and letters, for instance:

A Z B Y C X - what are the next two letters?

The second IQ portion had lots of squiggly lines or geometric shapes. The test displayed a set and asked which options shown should be next.

The last test was general knowledge of ATC. Good thing that one was not part of the grade overall – I had no idea on earth what frequency ranges aircraft used or what a VORTAC was!

The total time of the combined tests was four hours. As I walked out my brain was warm and throbbing in an unusual way – it felt like a muscle after being given a good workout.

About six weeks later I received a letter with my scores. The form letter attached indicated that although in general the federal government considered 70% to be a passing grade, no one would be placed on their list for possible employment as a controller unless their score was 90% or higher. I scored 98.7%.

Stress is Relative!

Downtown Indianapolis skyline circa 1979

Stress is Relative!

CHAPTER 3

Accepting the Challenge

There would be years of screening and training all while on the government's payroll before I was certified as a controller. Before the job was even offered I was required to visit the local FAA Flight Surgeon for a physical. Then I had to take a psychological exam and finally I would be interviewed by an Air Traffic Manager. While all that was going on my background would be examined by the FBI. The job carried a requirement for a "secret" clearance.

The physical was easy – at 27 years of age I did a lot of dancing and some modeling. My only worry was my eyesight. I have worn glasses since childhood, but my vision was correctable to 20/20 so it turned out all right. Apparently, my hearing was remarkable – all the way up and down the scale.

(I also have perfect pitch, but the hearing test never asked what notes they were playing!)

The psych Doctor asked various questions and I answered as honestly as I could. After he was done he called and made an appointment for me with a gentleman at the Indianapolis Air Route Traffic Control Center (ARTCC) so I guess he figured I wasn't crazy

Visiting Indianapolis Center was my very first look at what Air Traffic Control was all about, a world of new experiences and an exciting glimpse of what my life could be. I had to go through security,

Stress is Relative!

which in the days before 9/11 was much easier than it is today. The secretary at the reception desk buzzed me in the front door.

The deputy chief greeted me in a polite, professional manner. He guided me on a short tour of the facility. The controllers mostly ignored our presence as we toured the large, very dark room, containing large round radar scopes. There were two controllers sitting at each scope and another person taking paper strips off of a computer, placing them in a plastic holder and inserting them into a rack to the left of the radar scope.

A supervisor sat working at a desk behind us – he had a clear line of sight so he could keep up with what was happening on the active positions. The only woman I saw in the facility that day was the receptionist out front, all the controllers were men.

After that I sat with the manager in his office for about 30 minutes. He gave me a short description of what going through training would be like if I got in. He was impressed by my score so I was placed on the vetted list of candidates for the job.

Then I waited.

* * * * *

I told my parents about taking the test. They were not surprised that I'd scored well, though the idea of me working in that field was strange to them. No one in our family at the time was involved in aviation at all.

The information I received indicated that I would be sent to the FAA Academy as the first step in learning the job and that I'd be paid to go to school. In my mind this equated to going to school, and I had always enjoyed school.

Stress is Relative!

There was so much I did not know, and no way to know <u>what</u> I did not know! A person has to at least have a basic understanding of what is entailed to formulate intelligent questions.

What I did have was confidence in my ability to learn. I could step off into this new world and if I did fail I had a large, loving family who would help me recover emotionally and financially. With that kind of support I was ready to step up to the challenge.

Of course, we are talking about the federal government. The process was slow and I did not hear anything for a long time. I continued to do my job at the bank and although I hoped I'd be called, I did not make the mistake of packing too soon.

* * * * *

It was over five months later, in mid-July when I got the phone call. The workday had just begun – I had not yet drawn a cup of tea or turned on the old Selectric II typewriter when the phone rang. The FAA's hiring representative was named Dottie and I later learned that she was the one who called hundreds of people a year to offer them jobs.

Stress is Relative!

When she asked if I wanted a job at Albuquerque Center my first response was "What's a Center?" I had been interviewed at a tower, and saw the approach control…a Center was something different

Dottie said it was a large building with a lot of radars where traffic was controlled as it went across the country. She told me I would have to go to the Air Traffic Control Academy, and if I graduated from there I would be sent to Albuquerque. She told me how much I would earn, and that on top of that I would be given a stipend to cover living expenses while in training at the Academy.

I was to be given a salary of $17,500 per year while I was at the Academy. If I graduated I would immediately be bumped up to $21,000. At that point in time I was making $12,000 at the bank.

It was exciting, and scary, and the little voice we all carry in the back of our mind was jumping up and down screaming "Go for it!"

"Why not?" I thought.

I asked her if there were any jobs a little closer to Indianapolis. Not at that time, she said. I was told that air traffic control trainees were expected to go to their "first duty station" after the Academy to get their training and work for a while.

It would take about three years to be certified at Full Performance Level, and after that time I could bid on other facilities around the country. Since there was a Center in Indianapolis, I could bid back to the Midwest at that point if I desired to be closer to family.

It was an opportunity to attain a lucrative, respected job in a challenging field. I decided to go for it. The timing was good for the kids since they were on summer vacation and could stay in Indiana with my parents until I'd made housing and school arrangements in Oklahoma City.

Stress is Relative!

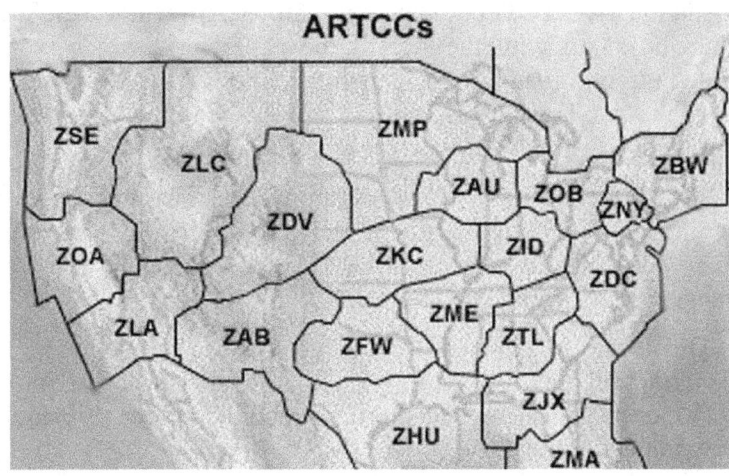

This map depicts the airspace boundaries of each Air Route Traffic Control Center across the nation.

There are times in life where you feel like you are hanging in mid-air being wafted from event to event. This was one of them. I was a girl from the Midwest, used to flat land covered in cornfields and vibrant green woodland areas with creeks. Anything west of the Mississippi would be a mystery and an adventure.

At that time women were not expected to take on jobs more challenging than secretary, school teacher, or nurse. Most were still expected to marry well and become mothers.

Defying the expectations of social groups in this era for what women were expected to do or be was never a conscious decision. Doors opened at critical times in my life and I simply walked through. It was not a career I had ever considered or even knew existed. Yet, without hesitation I said yes.

Stress is Relative!

    Frantically trying to think of anything else I'd need, I asked Dottie to send me a letter so I could get out of my apartment lease. She said it would be along with the rest of the paperwork, which would also include information on living accommodations in Oklahoma City – the site of the Air Traffic Academy. The FAA required I be there at 8am on August 1st – just two weeks away.

    As I hung up I sat and looked through the glass wall down and out over the large foyer of the bank for a bit. My mind immediately started flying through all the logistics of moving and what kind of arrangements I would need to make for the kids.

    Did I stop to think of what might happen if I failed to make it through training at the Academy? No, it just never occurred to me. A door opened and I stepped through, though I probably should have turned on the light first.

* * * * *

    I waited until my boss had had his morning coffee before quietly knocking on the doorframe. He waved me in and I sat down and gave him the news.

    He looked pained, then sighed and said "Do you see this?". He held up a piece of paper. "I was just recommending you for a raise…is there any way you'd consider staying?"

    I smiled and went over the numbers in my head. "Can the bank double my salary?"

    He just said "I wish I could."

* * * * *

    The news about the job did not surprise my parents – they knew my ATC test score. They both deserve a lot of credit because neither one ever said "But Rose, you don't know anything about airplanes." Or "Girls can't do that job."

Stress is Relative!

For the era they were very open minded about what their kids could do. Neither one had ever said us five girls had to get married, stay home and be moms/housewives. They encouraged us to take classes and get involved with things we were interested in.

The only thing they forbade based on gender happened when I was 13…up to that point I played football with all the other neighborhood kids – I was a pretty decent halfback. As I started to develop physically, they told me that I could only play flag football – how boring is that? I lost all interest in the game after that for a long time.

I was not the only one of the five girls in my family to wander away from traditional life pathways for women in the era. My sister, Bernadette went into the police Academy and eventually became a captain in the Indiana State Police. Donna was always into art – she learned all about printing and various visual art techniques and during her career has created beautiful, whimsical pieces which have sold internationally.

Susan went into medicine – she became a nurse and worked primarily in hospitals – in almost every department from emergency rooms to obstetrics to surgery. Loretta, the youngest, followed Mom's footsteps and became a payroll manager for a large multinational corporation.

I won't leave out my only brother. Karl was a pain in the butt as a pre-teen – having three older sisters bossing him around kinda irritated him. He went to college and found a natural talent for analysis and distribution management. You know those big semi-trucks you pass on the highway? He figured out where each has to go and what loads to put into them.

And now here I was heading off to become an Air Traffic Controller.

What did concern my parents was the distance away from home I would have to move. Albuquerque is over 1,200 miles from Indy. I have a pretty large family whom I love. Mom was afraid I would be homesick, but it just didn't even occur to me at the time. Later in life she told me she was amazed that I could just pick up and go.

Maybe moving would have been more difficult if "home" was a place, but for me it was people, specifically at that time my home was wherever the kids were, and they were transportable.

My life up to that point had pretty well prepared me to roam wherever I needed to be. Dad's job with United Home Life Insurance involved opening new offices in different states, so every year or so he and Mom would gather up all the kids and move. We finally settled in a house in Indy when I was about 13, but before that I had lived in 12 different places and three other states: Minnesota, Illinois and Kentucky. Being the oldest of six kids, I had moving down to an art.

(Number one priority – move the toilet paper first)

* * * * *

My artsy friends were the most astonished. It wasn't that they thought I couldn't do the job, they just didn't think I could divorce myself from the theater work I loved and had trained for since I was in grade school.

I remember telling the manager of the Booth Tarkington Civic Theater in Indianapolis, where I worked part time about the job. She looked at me like I was nuts and said "How can you just GIVE UP theater?"

Make no mistake, I loved performing, but at that point I did not see it as a viable way for me to support my children. When fate made me a mother, their needs took precedence. Until such time as they became independently functioning adults, I had to make sure they were loved and protected to the best of my ability. In my view, this job was an opportunity for me to fulfill that need.

Stress is Relative!

One of Rose's last roles performed before leaving for the Academy – Dulcinea in *Man of La Mancha*.

* * * * *

It wasn't as though the arts would be denied to me, they just took a backseat for awhile.

The next two weeks were a whirlwind of activity as I packed and moved out of my apartment and tried to guess what I would need with me in Oklahoma City and what should be left behind.

I decided that I did not need to move my furniture so it all went out in a garage sale. I would get new stuff whenever I settled. The old upright piano was sold – I think I missed it the most. Since the girls were seven and eight years old I gave the rocking chair to my sister, Susan, who was expecting.

Stress is Relative!

Mom and Dad agreed to keep the kids for the first week while I got settled in and arranged for schools. Later my sisters, Susan and Lori, drove the kids out to join me in Oklahoma.

* * * * *

From Indianapolis, take Interstate-70 to St. Louis, turn onto Hwy 44, which is partly toll road, all the way to Oklahoma City. At that time the world's largest McDonald's restaurant was situated on a structure that arched up over the top of I-44 – also known as Will Roger's Turnpike.

Since the highways from Albuquerque transition through OKC on the way to Indianapolis, I would drive that route about twice a year for the next thirty years.

While driving to Oklahoma City I reminisced about my life up to that point. As usual I sang at the top of my voice for a good deal of the trip, and listened to the radio or a cassette tape for part of it. And occasionally just wondered how my life was going to change.

* * * * *

The FAA Academy is big business in OKC, so there are a lot of furnished apartment complexes that cater primarily to its students. I chose a two bedroom apartment in one called the Railhead. It was pricier than some of the others but in a nice neighborhood and close to a day care center. It had a playground as well as a pool and there were some fast food places nearby. It was in a decent neighborhood – something that is very important to a single mom with small children.

You could get a lease for however long your classes would last – in my case three months.

Stress is Relative!

Billed as the "World's Largest" McDonalds Restaurant in 1983, the building straddles a four lane highway in southwestern Missouri.

Stress is Relative!

The Air Traffic Control Academy at Mike Monroney Aeronautical Center in Oklahoma City, Oklahoma.

CHAPTER 4

Entering on Duty at the Academy

It was a bright, sunny day on August 1, 1983, as I drove into the huge parking lot of the Academy. The Mike Monroney Aeronautical Center, which houses the Air Traffic Control Academy, is adjacent to Oklahoma City's Will Rogers Airport. The grounds were larger than many university campuses.

There were many large buildings and scattered through the area were unfamiliar structures I came to learn were antennas, radio towers and aviation equipment. In addition to controllers, the Academy taught all the FAA's communications and equipment technicians and every other related profession.

Walking across the pavement I saw license plates from every state in the continental U.S. plus Alaska. What I was about to enter was way bigger than just a job. I would be involved in a whole new community, meeting people from places I had never been, and working alongside them with a mission to give everyone a way to travel safely and quickly through the air.

Groups of people carrying the same type manila envelope that I was grasping in my right hand were moving towards the main administration building. Hitching my purse strap more securely over my shoulder I followed.

Stress is Relative!

A guide inside the door pointed the way to the auditorium where hundreds of people were searching for their assigned class numbers.

Halfway down the center aisle on my right, I found the number 83529. This number would represent a patchwork quilt of personalities from all over the United States brought here in the hopes of becoming a unique type of person – the air traffic controller.

Pushing a strand of hair back over my shoulder, I scooted into the row about three seats down. I had just settled my purse and papers in the right hand seat when a flurry of blond hair and blue eyes plopped down in the seat to my left.

"Hi." He had a big flashy smile with a definite hint of the Windy City in his voice. "Mind if I sit here?"

I smiled, amused, "Go right ahead."

"So-wa, have you found a roommate yet?"

"Way, way, wait a minute," this last coming from a brown haired young man seated behind me. He continued with, "this here is a lady, She don't wanna move in with no bum." I noticed he had very handsome brown eyes. He extended his hand. "Hi, I'm Tony."

The blond man slapped his hand away. "And I'm Rod."

I chuckled low over their antics and said. "Rose Kern."

"So... Rose," began the distinctive Clevelandish twang, "You gotta place yet?"

"Yes, thank you, I'm signing a lease this afternoon for a two bedroom apartment."

"Well, you know," Tony continued, "if you're in need of a partner to keep down the rent, I could help you feel real secure. You know, a girl all alone in a strange town...."

I shook my head, "Thanks, but I have two roomies already."

"Too bad, Tony, but such is life." Rod chimed in. "However, I wouldn't mind splitting the rent with someone."

Stress is Relative!

"Say no more my good man,' quipped Tony, "I have got just the place."

'And so,' thought I, 'is born what will undoubtedly become a unique partnership.'

The room filled rapidly during this exchange and we looked up upon hearing knocking coming from the stage. A middle-aged man in a three piece grey suit, the Academy's manager, was calling the assembly to order. I do not remember all he told us that first day, but here is the gist of it.

* * * * *

"Good morning, ladies and gentlemen." The speaker began. "And welcome to the Federal Aviation Academy."

"For most of you, the next three months will be an initiation into a whole new life. The job of air traffic controller is demanding, exacting work which will require you to learn a little of every facet of aviation science, its language and rules. The rewards are many, the training is intense.

Here at the Academy you will be put through a great many tests, some academic, and some working problems dealing with simulated aircraft. Your continued employment with the FAA will be based on the test scores we receive from you. Seventy percent is considered passing. Sixty-nine point nine, nine, nine....isn't."

He paused a moment to let that sink in, and I noticed a few other besides me who were sobered by the meaning of that sentence.

"Think he's trying to scare us?" queried Tony.

In a more encouraging manner the manager continued, "You should all be proud of the fact that you made it here. Out of 1,000 people who take the ATC exam less than ten percent make it this far. It is our experience that only about 40% of you here today will graduate and go on to continue training in the field at the facility you are assigned to."

Stress is Relative!

That was an interesting statistic…only 40% make it. It didn't scare me, but I was glad that I knew I had the support of my family in Indiana if things turned sour.

"While here in Oklahoma City you will be expected to maintain high standards of behavior and living conditions. We like for the citizens of this community to think of us as 'Good Neighbors'. You will receive expense money in advance to help in locating an apartment in town."

"Did you know they're going to give us a thousand bucks? Just for showing up!" Rod whispered.

"Shhhh!" I waved him to hush.

"…a great many stores hereabouts will cash your checks strictly on the basis of your FAA class number. A bounced check, an arrest for drunken driving, even unexcused tardiness can, and will, result in your dismissal from the Academy."

"For you single men a word of caution, there are a lot of young ladies in Oklahoma City who would really like to marry someone who makes the kind of money this career brings – and they get pregnant easily."

The manager walked out from behind the podium.

"Air Traffic Control is a profession that is respected throughout the world. I was a controller for over twenty years before coming to teach here at the Academy. I enjoyed the work, I enjoyed the money. It's a goal worth working toward. Welcome to the first step."

* * * * *

Halfway through the day, the thirty-six members of class 83529, and the eight other classes in the auditorium, were required to stand and take a pledge recited by those who protect the skies which among other things promises never to go on strike.

CHAPTER 5

Introductions

The rest of the day consisted of filling out all the endless insurance, security, and other miscellaneous forms required of new government employees. We lined up and went to a place where they gave us our first housing paycheck. Like Rod said - $1,000! That was more than I normally made in a month!

Then a trip to a crowded room where we were given a stack of books half as tall as a small horse. Since there were several classes all starting at the same time I wasn't sure which of the couple hundred people there I would be working with.

It was not until the next day I had a chance to meet some of the other 35 people in my group as they gathered in the classroom. It was a standard lecture hall with narrow tables and chairs on rising platforms. Being early, I chose a place in the 2nd row. There was a girl from central Wisconsin to my left who looked as nervous as I felt in these new surroundings.

Her name was Belle and she hailed from farm country in the central plains. She told me she had already glanced into the books we had been given and just as quickly shut them again. They were in a language we couldn't as yet begin to fathom. She also looked over the complex map of the hypothetical airspace in which the air traffic problems were to take place.

Stress is Relative!

One of the testing labs at the FAA Academy. Notice the racks containing strip holders. The strips contain information pertinent to each flight.

Like 97% of the population, including me, Belle figured air traffic controllers all worked at airports – she never really thought about what system was used to control aircraft already up and flying. So she was a little disappointed at first to discover that the rest of her career would take place in a huge darkened room – no windows, just radar.

A man and woman arrived together, though I decided from their manner that they weren't really a "couple". Barbara and Daren had both been stationed together at Keesler Air Force Base and were military controllers. I commented that this should all be very familiar to them..

Barbara grinned and glanced at Darin. "We'll see," she demurred.

Over the next few minutes a wide assortment of people wandered in. Tony and Rod looked like they had spent their housing money at a saloon, they crept over to the far right side of the room nd slumped over the long table.

Stress is Relative!

A tall, thin guy with dark wiry hair came in with his head down and one hand in a pocket. He cautiously looked up through black rimmed glasses. He seemed twitchy, probably just as nervous as the rest of us. He had an unusual name, but his habit of devouring candy bars and cokes seemed to make him constantly jittery, so the class called him Ziggy.

I had to admit that a significant portion of my class was comprised of fairly handsome men. Guess it was to be expected since they had all had to pass the physical to get in. There were 36 total in the class, only four of them were women.

We had a couple professional musicians in the group – drummer and saxophonist. There was a bright eyed young car salesman, and one guy who had been a professional instructor for a golf course.

A slender gawky blond guy walked in just behind someone who could have been a lineman for the Chicago Bears. Luke and Brad, who had decided to share room expenses while at the Academy.

Another girl walked in timidly and made her way to the back row in the corner. A self-styled cowboy swaggered in last complete with Stetson and boots.

There were four instructors sharing teaching duties for the first six weeks of our term: J.W. Larkin, Jock Johnston, Butch Morgan, and Drake Szusza. They never insisted on being called "Mr." We just used first names or nicknames from day one. Later on they would split the class in half, with two each guiding us through the simulation phase. They went over how the courses were structured in general, and gave us some personal advice.

"The FAA does not pay extra to study outside of these classrooms, and we can't tell you to do any homework. We can recommend you develop study groups – which will come in handy later on. "

"If any of you brought girlfriends, wives or kids with you, you might consider sending them back home…the next three months are going to be hard work and they will be a distraction." Several of the students frowned at that one.

Stress is Relative!

"Well," I thought, "That is just too bad." My daughters would be there by Saturday – not much choice when you are a single parent. Besides, I already missed Carrie and Missy. Over the next three months coming home to their hugs was what got me through. Heck, without them I don't think I would have made it. Kids are great stress relievers.

We were told there would be two phases of training. One was completely academic. The second was a series of simulations where we would be the controllers. The second phase was weighted higher than the first. After the last simulations were done there would be a final test. The combined scores of the academics, the simulations and the final test were averaged together and we would be given our final scores in private along with either a dismissal slip or orders to report into our first duty station.

We each received a copy of FAA Order 7110.65, an 8x10 book over an inch thick. This was, and is, the bible of Air Traffic Control. It has sections on procedures and requirements for Towers, Approaches, and Centers. We had to memorize all of it related to Center controlling.

Our first challenge was the language. J.W. explained the importance of always using the correct phraseology.

"All of you will learn to speak clearly using very specific terminology. You will learn when numbers should be stated separately and when they are allowed to be grouped and you will learn to spell out words using the aviation alphabet. The language of aviation is specific, stilted and formal. It evolved as a way to communicate over crackly, fuzzy radios. The pilots and controllers all give information in the same way and listen for specific phrases. Random conversation is the enemy of safety in ATC.

You will learn about all the components of the National Air Traffic system including all the flight characteristics of various aircraft, how the navigation equipment functions, what frequency ranges are used and how to interpret weather radar."

Stress is Relative!

The instructor went on. "You will also learn all the non-radar methods and procedures for controlling air traffic, and you will do it so well that you can tell aircraft where to go in your sleep."

Apparently radar training would not be part of the course – that fun subject is not taught until a year or two later after a person has been certified on all the non-radar positions. The only radar we needed to know was weather related.

"By the time you have finished your training you will know absolutely that whatever decision you make, whatever control instructions you give are correct. You will not doubt yourself because the pilots and passengers in the aircraft you speak to must be confident that they are safe in your hands."

The next instructor, Butch, had us open up a book with a lot of airplane pictures – small ones with one engine, medium sized ones with 4 or 5 windows per side, big ones like the air carries use and a lot of military ones. All of them had names and designators, like C172 stood for a Cessna model 172 – known as a Skyhawk. We had to memorize about a hundred of them by the end of the week.

He also went over the physics of flying, and how the various aircraft surfaces worked.

Lunch was available at the School's cafeterias, or people could bring their own and eat in the breakroom where the soda and candy machines stood. Each day we had a five minute break every hour and an hour for lunch.

That first day I ate quickly then wandered around a bit. The Academy had its own medical care center and a credit union. The credit union was in the main building and a very handy place to open a checking account. In those days online accounts were not even dreamed of – for that matter there were no such things as personal computers or cell phone!

* * * * *

Jock started the class after lunch by handing out even more sheets of paper – these were covered with groups of letters next to what looked like

Stress is Relative!

city names. "These are airport codes. Every airport in the nation has one. Large airports have three letters like LAX, NYC, or OKC. Smaller airports may be combined with numbers like 5V5 or 40CA".

"On Friday you will take a test covering the airports on these sheets of paper. Also, you will be expected to use the aviation phonetic alphabet when speaking in class and in the simulators."

I sighed as I thought of the hours of memorization facing me over the next three days. At least this was an area where my theater training would stand me in good stead. If I could memorize a play in three days then I should be able to handle a few hundred airport identifiers!

The last instructor, Drake, started us on learning how air navigation works. That an Airway is like a road in the sky – a set pathway between points - and went over the types of equipment used to navigate it. A navigational aid or NAVAID sends out radio signals that are picked up by equipment inside the aircraft.

NAVAIDs included non-directional radio beacons (NDB), TACANs, VORTACs and others. I made the classic beginner's error – I asked him a question about a VOR – I pronounced it "vore."

"A VORE is a Russian Whore" he obviously expected someone to make that error. Those in the class who did have an aviation background guffawed. "A Vee-Oh-AHR transmits radio waves in a 360 degree circle for aircraft to home in on."

It was a common beginner's mistake. TACAN is pronounced as a word, VORTAC is a word, but V-O-R must have all the letters stated individually.

OK, I got the "really feel stupid" award that day.

CHAPTER 6

The Study Group

From the literature sent in advance I found a good place to stay while I was in training at the Railhead Apartments. The large sprawling complex catered to the Air Traffic Academy's needs – completely furnished apartments with shuttle service to the Academy. It was conveniently located near a daycare where I could drop the girls off on my way in. The daycare had a school bus that took them to the local elementary school and at the end of my day I picked them up from the same location.

Most study groups consisted of four people – our teachers said it was the most convenient number for when we got to the simulations later on. I was the only female in my study group, and we all were staying at the same apartment complex. Two of the others were married guys – Dean and Mike.

Mike had heeded the advice and left his family behind. Personally, I have always thought that Mike would have done a lot better overall if they had been with him. He was a smart, motivated young man. He missed his wife and kids terribly, and since his wife was pregnant he worried all the time.

The other married one, Dean, had been a musician – classically trained. His wife visited often since they came from just a state away.

The fourth, Luke, was fresh from a college in Wisconsin. Slender and blond, he continuously displayed amusing turns of phrase. He would say he was going to the bubbler when he meant a drinking fountain. After a particularly grueling day he would widen his eyes and in a small voice whisper "I'm so CONFUSED….." in such a way that we would all crack up laughing.

Luke's roommate, Brad, was a large easy going guy who never bothered with study groups. His dad was an air traffic controller, so he had a leg up on the rest of us. Luke said Brad would go home to their apartment after the Academy and spend hours watching "The Beverly Hillbillies" and drinking Old Milwaukee beer.

* * * * *

I am going to stray a bit and talk about wives. This was the first time in my life I had worked in a field where over 90% of the people I worked with were male. I learned very quickly that any woman married to one of my classmates automatically looked at me, and any other woman in the job, as a potential rival.

Though I was single at the time, I was not looking for any kind of relationship – especially amongst a group of people I would either never see again in three months, or may be working with for years to come!

Nonetheless, I quickly mastered a technique that I think of as "friendly, but distant" as a shield against unwanted attention from both my male classmates and their wives. One of these days I may write an article for women in business on the subject.

Basically, I always dressed in business attire at work, or when participating in social events I dressed casually. No tight skirts, plunging necklines or four inch heels – nothing that "advertised". I was not there to "catch a man"!

In this place, at this time, I had come to build my own future and my own fortune. An early marriage and divorce was my wakeup call to the fact that the childhood ideal of a handsome prince riding up on a white horse who sweeps me into a big white wedding and provides financial and emotional stability for the rest of my life while I keep house and make babies is not only a fantasy, but a limiting concept of my role in life.

I needed to be able to take care of myself and my daughters. I wanted a career that was interesting and challenging. I required that my co-workers respect my knowledge, skills and abilities.

The image I created was one of competence and hands-off approachability. Friendly, but Distant.

* * * * *

During the first six weeks we studied aviation history, aircraft types, weather, and what all the components of the National Airspace System were from radar to airways. Until now, like most people, I had only seen the tall slender towers rising over an airport and the ARTCC where I'd been interviewed.

Now I learned that towers only control the aircraft on the airport surface and in the immediate vicinity aloft. Only larger airports have Approach Controls which monitor aircraft on RADAR as they transition in and out of airspace within about 30 miles and up to maybe 13,000 feet.

The facility I was being trained for was an Air Route Traffic Control Center, (ARTCC or "Center"). There are only 22 of these across the nation. They handle air traffic over very large geographic areas from the surface to 60,000 feet (over 11 miles up). I was destined for Albuquerque ARTCC which controls the airspace over New Mexico, Arizona and west Texas.

We learned the basics of how aircraft managed to fly in the atmosphere. At home I would sing the aviation alphabet to the tune all kids learn – and my kids sang it with me.

When I learned which components of an aircraft allowed it to turn, roll and climb or descend, I would envision my body as the aircraft. The girls and I would extend our arms – hands became ailerons, elbows were flaps and, of course, our butts were the rudders. We practiced "flying" around the living room.

* * * * *

Stress is Relative!

The girls did well in school. Back in Indiana Missy was in the second grade and Carrie in third grade. Carrie liked math and had started her multiplication tables – they both wrote in cursive. They surprised me the first day when Carrie told me her class was only doing simple addition and subtraction – and both girls were forced to go back to printing their letters!

Thank heaven it was only for three months, one way or another my kids would get back into schools that would challenge them, as soon as the Academy was done challenging me.

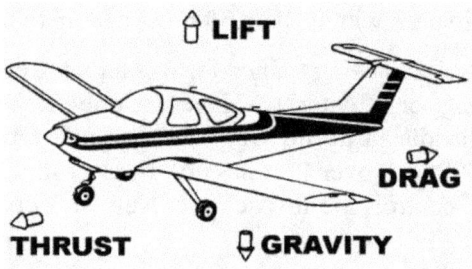

Stress is Relative!

Aviation Alphabet

A	Alpha	J	Juliet	S	Sierra
B	Bravo	K	Kilo	T	Tango
C	Charlie	L	Lima	U	Uniform
D	Delta	M	Mike	V	Victor
E	Echo	N	November	W	Whiskey
F	Foxtrot	O	Oscar	X	X-Ray
G	Gulf	P	Papa	Y	Yankee
H	Hotel	Q	Quebec	Z	Zulu
I	India	R	Romeo		

NUMBER pronunciations

1	One	11	one-one
2	Two	12	one-two
3	Tree	20	two zero
4	Fo-wah	100	one hundred
5	Fi-fe	1100	one thousand one hundred
6	Six	11000	one one thousand
7	Seven	11500	one one thousand five hundred
8	Eight	18000	one eight thousand
9	Niner	FL180	Flight Level One eight zero
10	One Zero		

Civilian aircraft – numbers/letters pronounced separately:
  N123RT – November one two three rome<u>o tango</u>

Military spoken in separate digits :
  R23456 – Army two tree fo-wah fi-fe six
  GHOST69 – GHOST six niner

Air Carriers – spoken in group form: DLA1236 – Delta twelve thirty six

Stress is Relative!

CHAPTER 7

Academics

In my class very few people actually came from aviation backgrounds. I think only two out of the 36 in our class had been pilots, three had been military controllers in the air force and one had a parent who worked in an ARTCC. So, learning not just the language but gaining understanding of how the entirety of the National Airspace System worked was challenging.

The sky is not a haphazard overlapping of aircraft flying off in every direction and altitude over the United States. There are rules created over the past 70 years since World War I defining which aircraft must fly at which altitudes and in what directions. There are places no one is allowed to fly over or even near.

There were hundreds of airport identifiers to memorize and some of them were strange. The easy ones were recognizable – LAX for Los Angeles, RNO for Reno, IND for Indianapolis. Others did not seem to have rhyme or reason – unless you were very familiar with the history of the area.

For example **APA** is the identifier for Centennial Airport in Denver. There was a time when it was smaller and had the name Arapahoe County Airport – named after the Native American Tribe who once lived in the area. Now APA makes more sense and sticks in the brain better.

Stress is Relative!

The names of military air bases are especially challenging – especially the navy. All of theirs begin with an N. NBG – Navy New Orleans, NKX-Miramar, NGZ-Alameda. When the teachers were out of the room we sometimes talked about them – coming up with elaborate ways to remember them. For instance:

NBG: Navy New Orleans. We decided that since the New Orleans Saints were having a winning season that year, the fans did not have to wear bags on their heads…so NBG was short for NO BAGS at Navy New Orleans.

NGZ: Navy Alameda. That was a stumper. Then Luke piped up "I know, it's for Gomez!" We looked at him strangely and he went on to say. "My buddy is in the Navy there – his name is Gomez Alameda." After that everyone remembered NGZ was where Gomez Alameda – Luke's fictitious buddy lived.

BE35 – Beechcraft Bonanza V-Tail

The aircraft types were equally a mystery. We were expected to memorize the names, identifiers and characteristics of about 50 different kinds – small to large propeller and jet aircraft, civilian and military, and helicopters.

Stress is Relative!

Our textbooks had the pictures with performance characteristics and manufacturer information for each aircraft. You could tell a Cessna by its high wings pretty easy. Beechcraft and Pipers looked a lot alike unless they had a distinguishing characteristic – like the Beechcraft Bonanza's V-tail.

Mooney aircraft look like someone pasted their tails on backwards – we called them Gooney Mooneys.

MO20 – Mooney

One thing that helped is that the tests used exactly the same pictures as in the textbook. So if two different twin engine propeller aircraft had three side windows and a stripe, but one was photographed in front of a building, then the building was the clue as to which aircraft it was.

* * * * *

The first day in class we were told we had to wear business casual clothing – no blue jeans were allowed. Most of my work wardrobe was office appropriate.

One day I came in wearing a dress made of blue polyester which resembled denim blue jean material. I had worn it a lot while working at the bank. The instructor sent me to the Human Resources office where I

Stress is Relative!

was told that since it looked like blue jean material it was not allowed and if I wore it again I would be dismissed.

Wow! That was unexpected.

In any situation, appearances matter. In this job you garnered more respect if you look competent and capable. Most of the instructors and staff at the Academy came from a military background.

Of course in those days they wore ties and jackets unless it was very hot. My hair was worn up in a bun, or chignon most of the time, and knee length skirts or dresses. Practical pumps with a bare inch high heel gave my short 5'3" height a small lift. In those days the style for eyeglasses included large frames.

* * * * *

The Aviation Weather Course introduced us to another whole new world of terminology: Coriolis forces, convective activity, AIRMETs, turbulence. It was the first time in my life I had thought about icing in the air.

Meteorology as related to aircraft was fascinating. The National Weather Service has a huge division solely devoted to observing and forecasting weather both surface and aloft as it relates to aviation. We had to learn how various kinds of aircraft handled different types of weather and how wind direction and speeds affected travel times and fuel consumption.

Tests were given almost every day. All the scores were kept to be totaled and averaged on the last day. For six weeks we studied the academics. We were supposed to have a five-minute break every hour, and half an hour for lunch.

Stress is Relative!

There were two large cafeterias on the grounds, as well as the FAA Credit Union, a small gift shop, and the administrative offices.

There was a grand hallway/foyer facing the street in the front near the classrooms containing many foreign flags. I learned from the plaques on the wall that the U.S. was the first country to develop an Air Traffic Control system and other countries sent their controllers to this Academy to learn our techniques. It was a pleasant place to relax with benches scattered around the room.

There was also a building for the Civil Aeronautics Medical Institute. CAMI housed an urgent care center, but mostly the residents were researching anything related to how aviation affected pilots, controllers and others in the industry. They were constantly trying to figure out what qualities made the best air traffic controllers.

Civil Aviation Medical Institute (CAMI)

Stress is Relative!

To that end, every single test we took had a few "CAMI" questions added. These questions were not counted in the test score, but you never knew which ones they were. They always related to the material we studied. Sometimes they mirrored a question elsewhere in the test, but phrased slightly differently.

I wonder if they ever figured out exactly what kind of person to look for. Over the last thirty years I have met a LOT of different types. Some were degreed professionals, some were businessmen or blue collar workers, and many were ex-military. There were a few that I simply think of as backwoods rednecks. All kinds of people do well in the job, but only if they can "see" traffic. I'll go into what that means later.

* * * * *

The federal government distributes payroll on every other Tuesday and I remember how ecstatic I felt at receiving the first paycheck while at the academy.

I began working at age 16 in my father's company as a secretary/receptionist and had attended some college prior to and during my first marriage. Once I got pregnant I stayed home, though I was really wanting to continue a career. My husband at the time told me that because I was a woman I wouldn't make enough money to pay for the babysitting.

So here I am looking at a paycheck almost double what he made at the time and knowing that if I continued doing well that my salary would only increase as I succeeded.

A bubble of amusement built up in my chest until I laughed at the irony.

* * * * *

Stress is Relative!

About three weeks into training one of the instructors, J.W., pulled me aside.

"Rose, I understand you have your children here with you?"

"Yes, Sir."

J.W. looked uncomfortable, but I could see he was sincerely concerned. "I know you've heard this before, but I want to urge you to find a family member or someone to send them to before you go into the simulations. Once that starts you cannot afford any form of distraction."

I smiled. "Thank you for the advice, but I don't have the option". He nodded and turned away.

I didn't mention that even if I did feel the option was available, I probably would not exercise it. I still think the only way I got through the next two months was because I had unlimited hugs to go home to each night.

* * * *

During the academic portion of the training the instructors were very generous in their hints as to what was on the tests. We would come to a portion of the class and one of them would stamp their foot loudly then stare at us all as if to say "Remember this, it is important!"

In almost every phase of training I have ever gone through, the FAA's attitude is that the academics, while necessary, are secondary to finding those people capable of doing the job. Simulations were taken far more seriously than book learning.

Stress is Relative!

CHAPTER 8

The Practice Simulations

Everyone in our class made it through the academics. Towards the end we were given a map to memorize – it was a chart similar to the ones that would show real aviation navigational fixes and airways, but simpler.

We were to assume we worked in "AERO Center" – the place names and aviation identifiers were similar to those in central Oklahoma. It used familiar place names like Tulsa, McAlester and Enid, but the airways and other information on the maps was not the same as in the real world. Aero Center was a simplified version of what the real world maps would be like if we made it through the Academy.

The map given to us would be used as the base for all the simulations in the last six weeks of training. The non-radar techniques we were trained to use depended on our knowing those radials by heart.

Sometimes an airport had one or more navigational fixes (NAVAIDS) that may or may not have the same name as the airport. For instance, OKC stood for both the airport and the navigational fix (VORTAC) in Oklahoma City, but in Roswell, New Mexico the airport is ROW, but the navigational aid located on the airport grounds is CME (Chisum).

Lines stretching from one VORTAC to another represent airways. (Airways are like streets in the sky, defined pathways from place to place)

Stress is Relative!

Each airway was named and we had to memorize the radials which comprised the airway.

For example, each VORTAC sent out a signal in a 360 degree circle. Low altitude airways were always "VICTOR" airways, so V12 was stated as victor twelve and it traveled off of the PNC (Ponca City) VORTAC 094 degree radial to the OKC VORTAC 265 degree radial.

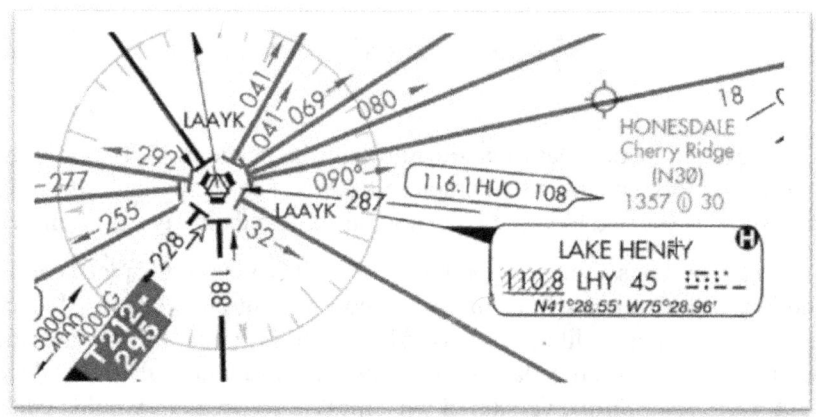

From a piece of paper with only spots representing the VORTACs we had to draw all the airways and label them with names and what radials they sprung from. We had to include all the other navigational aids and airports in AERO center, label other ATC facilities like approach controls and their frequencies. We also labeled any restricted airspace and the altitudes it included.

One of my classmates, the ex-Air Force guy, Darin, complained a lot about having to learn non-radar techniques. He had been a tower controller in the military and apparently they were trained using radar right away. I never asked him what they did if there was a power outage, or if their equipment went down for some reason.

Stress is Relative!

In the civilian environment the techniques developed over several decades prior to the implementation of radar were still taught – just in case. Apparently the differences between their Air Force training and the non-radar requirements of civilian Air Traffic Academy training became a big liability during the simulation portion of the training.

* * * * *

After the academics were over our original class of 36 was divided into two groups of 18 each. This was done because you could only test nine people at a time on the simulators so scheduling the classes separately was easier.

I don't know how the division of students was accomplished. It was not done by dividing in half an alphabetical listing of last names. I was surprised to note that the classes appeared to be lopsided. Butch and Jock were now leading a class which was composed entirely of white males. J.W. and Drake had all the women, the one African American man, one Hispanic, and one who came across as effeminate. The rest of the group was filled out with standard Caucasian middle class looking men.

During the first six weeks the whole group had become friendly in the way that disparate individuals who have come together for a purpose will. We played volleyball together on weekends and had gone out for a few meals.

When the class split up, the guys in the other group told us their teachers were giving hints and tips about upcoming simulation tests. At first some of those guys would pass them on to guys in our group, who might mention them to some of us.

The teachers for my group, J.W. and Drake, were pretty upright guys. They did not give out hints/tips, but answered questions put to them as best as they could. They were friendly but always seemed like they wanted us to succeed on our own.

Stress is Relative!

The other two, Butch and Jock, seemed bound and determined that their group of homogenous white males would ALL make it through..

For the first time in my life I became aware of a prejudice based on sex. Always before if I excelled at something I had been encouraged to pursue it by my parents – later on I found out how rare that was in my generation for women. Heck, all my siblings, boys and girls, went on to have very diverse careers. But in the early 1980's the current regulations about equal rights were more of a concept than a reality.

Luckily the four in my study group remained in the same class together. The study groups became intense once simulations started. Almost every night we were sitting in my apartment doing role playing. If I was the controller, someone else was a pilot, another was a different air traffic facility and the last one took notes. We would make up situations based on the ones we were given during the day at the Academy.

Because I had kids with me the group was kind enough to use my living room as our practice area. The girls were great during all this. They had homework themselves and played together while the adults practiced. I cannot say enough how wonderful my daughters are and how they really helped me get through everything.

Points were taken for errors in phraseology, procedures and separation. Each phraseology error was five points. Each procedure cost 10 points and if a separation error occurred it was 25 points – an automatic failure.

* * * * *

At the Academy during the first two weeks we practiced at least twice a day in a long room containing nine workstations. We had headsets, maps, and strips of paper containing the routes and altitudes of various aircraft. Unlike the real world, we would start with empty airspace and wait for the "pilots" to call as they were transitioning into the airspace. The people who pretended to be pilots were in the next room – they were referred to as "remotes".

Stress is Relative!

Sitting on a tall stool behind each one of us was an individual who had been an air traffic controller until he retired and came to work at the Academy. The evaluators had a clipboard, scorecard and a pen. They were also wearing headphones and could hear both the remote's transmissions and yours. If you made the slightest error it was noted. During the first two weeks they would give friendly advice as we were working out how to do the job, but once the graded simulations began, they never said a word.

I have never felt particularly comfortable about having someone looking over my shoulder while taking tests. I remember in high school I was taking a test in biology and the teacher was wandering through the room. She stopped behind me. It was not a particularly hard test and I had been whipping through it pretty well, but when she stood behind me all the muscles in my neck tightened up and I had a faint burning sensation rippling down from the crown of my head.

My pen stopped, as did my brain. After a couple minutes, I turned and looked up at her and said, "I'm sorry but I can't think with you right behind me." Luckily she took it well, smiled and moved on.

So here I was with someone parked right behind me – I had to get over the tendency to freeze up REALLY fast. I had never had stage fright – heck I spent years singing and acting. But on stage the audience is always out front, not breathing down your neck. *Ok, so, focus on the problem, pretend that guy with the clipboard isn't there. Breathe.*

The other class was on an opposite schedule to ours. One week they would do the simulations in the morning and we would do them in the afternoon, the next week we would switch. I guess the FAA was getting us used to the idea that in this career you never work a straight day shift - aircraft fly at all hours.

Each simulation lasted 20 to 30 minutes, and we all worked the same one – same calls signs, same situation over the same area of the sky. We wore headsets which helped to reduce the confusion of the other people around you all speaking at the same time. What added to confusion was that all of us were saying the same things generally – if you said something

Stress is Relative!

different than the ones on either side of you it meant that maybe you did not read the situation correctly….or they didn't.

A flight strip and a map and a good imagination were the tools. The flight strips gave the calls signs of the aircraft, the type aircraft, its airspeed, altitude and route of flight. It also gave an estimate as to when the aircraft would reach a specific place, or "fix". During the simulation there would be times when more than one aircraft would be in the same place at the same time at the same altitude. We had to correctly determine which aircraft, then figure out how to separate them.

Of course we were supposed to try to do this with a minimum of changes to the aircraft's altitudes or flight path. That is where errors in procedures could come in. The easy way to fix things would be to always make one aircraft climb or descend to a different altitude. But in reality pilots want to fly at the altitude the aircraft performs best at, so changing altitudes is supposed to be the last used choice.

The flight strips might show two aircraft on the same route at the same altitude, but the one trailing is faster. You might initially have all the aircraft separated but the remote pilot will call and request a change in altitude that now will bring him into conflict with other aircraft. As you calculate when each aircraft is reaching the boundary of your airspace you must have them contact the next sector.

Sometimes aircraft at the same altitude approached a fix from two different directions, but their estimated time of arrival at that fix was within a minute of each other – rules require a five minute difference. We were taught how to give instructions to one of them that would arc the aircraft around the fix.

Aircraft flying east or north are required to be at even altitudes; south and westbound aircraft are on odd altitudes. When we found one flying "Wrong Altitude For Direction of Flight", we were supposed to correct it. However, sometimes it was easier to let that aircraft stay at that altitude, but we either had to put them back on the correct altitude before they left our sector, or request approval from the next sector (APREQ) for it to stay WAFDOF.

Stress is Relative!

We might have someone at a high altitude that wanted to land in our sector, and of course there were aircraft in his way. By the same token, someone taking off had to be worked up to his requested altitude through traffic.

Since we had no radar, all this had to be done in your mind…keeping track of where each aircraft was. This is the essence of "seeing traffic." We had to visualize the location of each aircraft in three dimensions and determine where they would be in the next minute, and the minute after that.

> **This is the essence of "seeing" traffic.**

The aircraft were traveling at speeds that were equivalent to between four and eight miles a minute. They did not stay at the altitude you saw them on initially – as they reached their destinations they had to be worked down through the altitudes of the other aircraft safely and handed off to the tower or approach controller, or one of those entities would "give" you an aircraft climbing up into your airspace.

We marked up the flight strips with changes and pulled them off the board as the aircraft left our airspace. Each of us was issued a special mechanical pencil that had black or blue lead on one side and red on the other. Adding new information was done in blue/black and the red was used to correct information.

Stress is Relative!

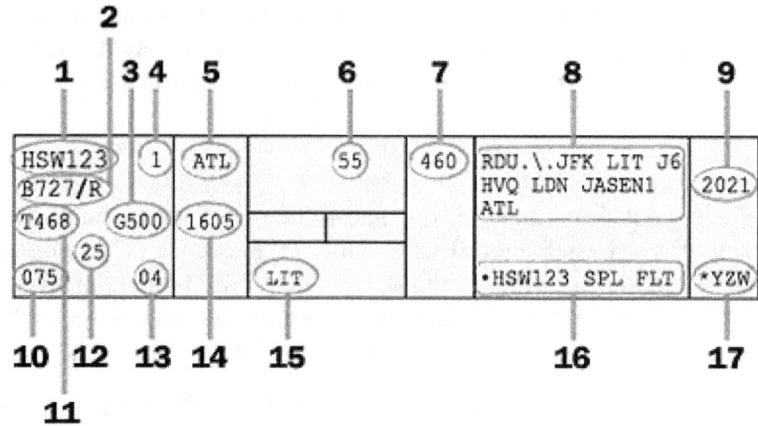

1. Aircraft call sign.
2. Type of aircraft/type of equipment.
3. Actual speed across ground.
4. Number of amendments to original flight plan.
5. The previous fix. This denotes where the aircraft has been.
6. Time aircraft is estimated to cross LIT.
7. The altitude at which the aircraft is flying. This is measured in feet. Multiply this number by 100 to give the altitude.
8. Flight route. This must show departure and destination points. This can be abbreviated before entering your facility airspace.
9. Individual beacon code assigned to each aircraft
10. Computer generated number for identification within this facility.
11. Filed true air speed
12. The sector number. This identifies in which sector the aircraft is flying.
13. The strip number. The number of strips printed for this flight in this center.
14. Time aircraft crossed previous fix.
15. Coordination fix for this strip.
16. Remarks area (The only place where free text can be entered)
17. Coordination symbol to adjacent ATC facility.

Stress is Relative!

We marked up the flight strips with changes and pulled them off the board as the aircraft left our airspace. Each of us was issued a special mechanical pencil that had black or blue lead on one side and red on the other. Adding new information was done in blue/black and the red was used to correct information.

Certain symbols – memorized from the handbook – were written as altitudes or routes were changed. Frequencies given were added to the strip. As aircraft reported over a fix the times had to be calculated and updated. As the aircraft exited our airspace you took down the paper strip with all the markings and threw it away. Those strips were then called "deadwood".

The first simulations were fairly easy – just a few aircraft. Of course the problems got more complex as time went on. As Luke came out of the simulation room one day I asked how he did. Luke said ruefully, "It rained aluminum all over McAlester".

* * * * *

Joking like that is how we kept our sanity. Yes, you know that when you are doing the job it's not just a game, those aren't empty drones traveling at 480 miles per hour. There will be hundreds of people inside each one who have given their trust to the pilot and to the air traffic system. You know that the decisions you make must keep those people safe all the way to their destination.

But any high stress job has to have its moments of humor – that is how humans balance the stress and keep their perspectives.

Stress is Relative!

CHAPTER 9

Downtime

The dynamics of the class changed somewhat after we were split into two groups. It was pure luck that my study group members all managed to remain in the same class.

Since no one knew anyone else in Oklahoma City, both classes frequently met at local restaurants on weekends or got together at someone's apartment complex clubhouse. The Railhead had a volleyball net out back and a pool.

There was a crazy restaurant called Molly Murphy's House of Ill Repute where the wait staff dressed up as movie characters and had to stay "in character" while they waited on you. The interior of the place was a hodgepodge of styles. Several of my classmates and I decided to try the place out one evening.

Our waiter was a big guy in leotards and a tutu who jumped on the table to take our order. There were ten of us there and we ordered a "feast" – which meant they brought out a big platter of grilled steaks and bowls of veggies and we speared what we wanted to eat and set it on our plates.

Some of the young, single guys would spend time at a strip joint called the Red Garter where the girls did a dance called "The Gaither". A few times we went to a big place where they had pool tables and video games. I beat all opponents on a video game called *Galaga*.

Stress is Relative!

I didn't really get any negative comments from my classmates at that time. Some of them I considered friends, others were just acquaintances you saw every day. They pretty much treated me like everyone else. One of the girls, the ex-military controller, Barbara, had to leave the training program because of a family emergency. I understand she came back in a later class.

* * * * *

All of the members of both classes would be assigned to Albuquerque Center if they made it through the Academy. I had read a little bit about Albuquerque – it was described as "High Desert". That was a tad daunting – after all I was a girl from the lush green Midwest and I was going to the desert? I had no idea if they even had trees there. That was in the days before personal computers and internet when you can look up everything. I just had an atlas – and my mental picture of "desert" was sand dunes and cactus.

Three of the guys in our group were pilots – so one extended weekend (Veteran's Day) they rented a small Cessna and flew to Albuquerque International airport. They loved it – they gave us all descriptions of the city and the beautiful mountains surrounding it.

One of them, Luke, from my study group, was from a flat green area in Wisconsin, and he was fascinated by the rocks lining the mountainside. He said they were as big as cars and they were just balanced in a way that looked like they would tilt over and roll downhill if you slapped them.

Yes, there were trees, but not much grass. The landscape was mostly rocks and cactus. They brought back some information on apartments and a city map for the rest of us to look over.

Of course, it was all pie in the sky until we graduated.

* * * * *

Stress is Relative!

When we began the simulations, our class had to share time with other classes – so we moved from just doing day shifts to every other week evening shifts. That played havoc with my childcare schedules. Luckily one other class mate had his wife and small kids there. She agreed to watch the girls when I had to work evenings.

Overall it was amazing that I so easily found schools, accommodations and good child care during this period – I continuously felt that this was the path fate intended for me.

.

Rose in the Simulation Room at the FAA Academy

CHAPTER 10

Graded Simulations Begin

The Academy was moving thousands of people in and out of the training every year. It was all a big screening process. They start you slow, but since they were trying to see how well you handled stress, there is no wonder that we were put on different time schedules. I was grateful they did not go so far as to demand we work midnight shifts, especially as the graded simulations were on our doorstep

The atmosphere was different the day we started the graded simulations. Everything was exactly the same as in practice as far as the locations, the personnel, and the set up were concerned, but the knowledge that what you did here would count for the bulk of your final score – and whether or not you kept the job – added a palpable underlying tension.

The biggest difference in the graded simulations was the recorders. Every word you said would be available later in case there were disputes concerning the scores afterwards. Here is where the hours spend practicing the language and procedures would pay off. Every word had to be precise; every instruction had to meet the required parameters.

The men scoring us were not allowed to speak to us or give pointers afterwards as they had during the practice simulations. The same set of instructors were now our evaluators but now they sat quietly behind us. I had grown somewhat used to them being there and was mostly able to block out the uneasiness of having someone behind me. Once the

Stress is Relative!

simulation started I was ok, I focused everything on what was in front of me.

We sat down to a strip board that was already loaded with aircraft supposedly already in flight. The strips contained the route, altitudes and airspeed data – the clock was set to match the time period on the strips. During the simulation new strips would be introduced and I was required to pull down the deadwood as aircraft left my airspace.

A copy of the Aero Center map with all the frequencies, airways and VORTAC radials was overhead in case I needed to glance up and see it, but it was better and faster if you could spit out the information without having to review the details. Having that information solid in your mind was a huge advantage. Here is where all that memorization came in handy.

The first simulation began with four aircraft already flying in my airspace. The strips in the proposal bay indicated that there would be four more entering over the next half hour. The timing on the ones already there told me how soon I had to initiate coordination for them with the next controller. I immediately saw where there could be two potential conflicts unless something was done.

I put on my headset and adjusted the microphone tube. As the clock turned the minute, a Remote, pretending to be an aircraft called as he was entering my airspace. I barely remember exactly what I did during each of the problems, just the stimulation of the quick decision making process.

The moment it was done I sat back and took a deep breath then turned to my evaluator who was writing something on his clipboard like all the others. He looked up at me and said. "Ok, I show one phraseology error, but otherwise, well done." I had a score of 95% on that one. Whew!

The tests were given every two days with classroom time in between while other classes were taking their tests. Like everything so far, each test was progressively harder. Apparently there were a lot of these pre-arranged simulations and you could not ask someone from another class what occurred if theirs was first because each class was given different ones of basically the same level of complexity.

Stress is Relative!

Only the instructors had been around long enough to know all of them and which ones would be given to which class.

* * * * *

This was where the biggest differences in our instructors came out. The students in our sister class were telling the guys in my class that their teachers were giving big hints on what was coming up in the simulations – when and where the problems were designed to have aircraft come into conflict.

Knowing that information in advance allowed them to go through separation techniques in their head prior to the test. Because many members of the other class had become friends with our class during the initial weeks, we sometimes got information passed down from them, but not always.

In my class the instructors played strictly by the book. You could ask them anything related to procedures or simulation logistics, but they would not give you any hints about what was upcoming.

In the other, all male class, the instructors gave hints and tips. None of us was familiar enough with the FAA to know what, if anything, could be done about that, plus if anyone from my class went to the Human Relations office it might reflect badly on us – or the other class. Plus we had no proof other than word of mouth.

* * * * *

I had gotten through five graded simulations with no separation errors – just a few phraseology and procedural ones. A few minutes before the sixth graded simulation one of the instructors from the other class, Jock, found me outside the area and said he wanted to talk to me.

He drew me away from anyone's hearing and said, "Rose, I have been watching you, you're pretty good at this."

Of course I was flattered and said thank you.

"I wanted to give you a little heads up about the next problem."

Stress is Relative!

This was new! To my knowledge neither of the instructors in the other class had volunteered any inside information to people in my class.

He went on. "The crux of the problem will be a pile up of aircraft over the top of the Enid VORTAC." He leaned in and stared at me. "The only way to get through the problem is to arc an aircraft south of the VORTAC, you got that?"

I acknowledged it and hurried into the classroom to get set up for the test.

* * * * *

Shortly afterwards my class went into the lab and readied themselves. Quickly I scanned the flight strips to get the picture in my head. Sure enough, there were going to be four aircraft heading towards the Enid VORTAC from various directions at conflicting altitudes But then I glanced up at the map over the position and realized what was really going on.

On the map, south of the airways around Enid was a restricted area. Restricted airspace is like a big rock in the sky. No civilian aircraft are allowed there. Routing an aircraft into it was an automatic separation error – an automatic fail. Jock had counseled me to do just that. He was deliberately setting me up.

As the problem started I did arc an aircraft around the Enid VORTAC, but I went north instead of south. I passed the simulation.

Now I had a dilemma. Should I report Jock? To whom? I didn't have any proof that he told me to do something that would make me fail. I was angry but my job was on the line. Did I really want to make waves at this point? I had passed the problem because I applied all the rules I had been taught correctly after assessing the situation on my own, not automatically doing what someone told me to do.

* * * * *

Stress is Relative!

It was the first time I ever encountered someone who WANTED me to fail and who went out of his way to do something about it. I never thought that I would ever fail just because I was a girl and it was a surprise to think that others thought I should.

Of course, in a way it was a mark of fear on the part of the person putting stumbling blocks in my way. If they were right and women were not smart enough to do the job, then I would never succeed to begin with. The fact that they had to try and trip me up meant that their small egos were threatened.

In the end I told no one. I had no proof. If confronted Jock could refute my statement, or he might even say that he meant to tell me north instead of south because he was trying to help.

I kept the incident to myself and to this day wonder what else I could have done. This was the first of many similar ethical dilemmas I would face during the course of my career.

Of course, I did do the one thing that he feared the most. I succeeded.

> **I did the one thing that he feared the most.**
>
> **I succeeded.**

Stress is Relative!

CHAPTER 11

The Stress

It was during this period when the stress of constant evaluation began to get to people. We heard rumors of a guy from a different class who committed suicide. He kept failing the simulations, but since he always had the option of just quitting, why did he choose to take his own life?

The story sobered us all and there were some discussions about what everyone would do if they failed. The statistics quoted to us that first day came back to us. Only 40% of those who came to the Academy made it through the initial training. Who among us would not be going on to Albuquerque?

I thought about my folks. I knew they would be disappointed for me, but I also knew they would be sympathetic if I did not make it. I was lucky that I had options. My old boss would welcome me back if I returned home to Indianapolis, or I could take time to reassess my life and try another pathway.

Some of my classmates had fall back plans, but some were basing their entire future on what happened there in Oklahoma City. Mike was especially affected by the stress. His pregnant wife was within a few weeks of her due date. She was home in Alabama with their three kids and lived close to her parents, but you could tell he was having a hard time focusing. I still think he was one who should have brought his family out

Stress is Relative!

to OKC – he really needed the solid confidence having family around you instilled.

Belle grew distant – her easy chattering ceased and she kept to herself. You couldn't tell if Ziggy was nervous – he'd been twitchy since day one. Dean and Jeff seemed to be holding their own and Luke reported that his roommate was still coming home after class with a take-out dinner and watching *Beverly Hillbillies* every day.

One member of our class bowed out halfway through the simulations. He just did not show up one day. We heard through the teachers that he had resigned. Most of those who were not doing well decided to stay the course until the last moment. Many of them, like Mike, were staying in cheap locations and pocketing the generous living allowance called "per diem" which was given to us on top of our salary to have as a cushion if things fell apart. Mike was sending every penny he could back to his wife.

Overall, I was holding my own. I had my girls, and early on we found an interesting church, St. Patrick's, where we attended Sunday Mass. Prayer or meditation or just taking time to sit and breath and do honest but gentle self-assessment helps me get through stressful times.

Getting through ATC school was not just about me. It was one way of showing my daughters they could and should strive for what they wanted in life even if others didn't think they should or could.

Carrie and Missy both were still doing very well in school – too well. If we had had to stay longer than three months in Oklahoma I would have pushed for them both to be advanced a grade, but our time there was growing short.

CHAPTER 12

The Final Exam

The simulations were done and only one test was left before all the scores on all the tests we took since day one were combined and a grade given out which would determine whether we were employed or not.

The night before the test we broke out all the old texts from the first set of classes months before. That information would be on the test as was the separation information we had been utilizing during the simulations.

Most people had a general idea of how well they had been doing. Some had kept meticulous records and knew what grade they needed on the final test to average a score of 70% or better over the 3 months we were there. This last test was weighted fairly heavily and some people were praying for a high score to bring up their average.

I pulled everything out and went over it as well, but didn't really worry about it. I had been holding my own, and like I said earlier – I am really good at tests. My scores in the simulations were not bad – I had failed a couple of the later ones, but I knew that as long as I scored 52% or higher on the final test I would managed a final grade of 70% and still stay employed.

Like all the others it was a multiple-choice exam with God knows how many CAMI questions in the mix. It took well over an hour.

Stress is Relative!

* * * * *

After we turned the tests in, we were instructed to turn in our textbooks. We would receive our results the next day at which time we would either be given the orders for our new assignment, or our employment would be terminated.

That night the girls and I packed up everything. One way or another we would be leaving the next day and either head east to Indianapolis, or west to Albuquerque. There was not much to pack other than clothes and a few toys and books. I had given Railhead my notice, the next afternoon I would drop off the key.

The next day we went back to the classroom we had started in so many months earlier. The teachers came in with a stack of papers. They told us it had been nice working with all of us, and told us that after we received our grades we should make our way to one of two places.

If the final score was 70% or higher we went to an office that gave us paperwork to take to our next duty station plus a $1,000 check to cover moving expenses. If it was less than 70% we went to a different office for out processing. If any of us wanted to dispute the final grade there was a third office we should go to where all our old test scores and the audio tapes from our simulations would be re-evaluated.

Our scoresheets were in envelopes with our names on the outside. It was easy to tell those who made it from those who did not. In my study group Dean and Luke made it, but I will never forget the look on Mike's face when he saw the final grade. It was heartbreaking.

Belle was furious. Her grade was 69.7%. She asked the instructors if anything could be done and they sent her to the re-evaluation office. Later I heard that her final score was actually lowered as small errors not previously caught by the simulation evaluators were noted on the re-evaluation.

Stress is Relative!

The ex-military guy from our class, Dean, made it by a hair. He'd had a hard time adjusting to civilian practices. Luke's *Beverly Hillbilly* loving roommate, Brad, sailed through with a 97%.

My final score was 82.5%. Not the best grade, but more than enough.

When it all settled out I was not surprised to see that every member of the all-white-male sister class made it through, where my class had about a 33% success rate. No one in our class made it who was not Caucasian and I was the only woman to pass.

I remember wondering if Belle or any of those others who did not fit the straight white male stereotype had had one of the other instructors sidle up and give them false "advice" before a simulation. If so, none of them mentioned it.

A total of 24 of the original 36 would be making their way down Interstate 40 to Albuquerque over the next few days. We had won the right to continue our training for one of the nation's most prestigious government careers- Air Traffic Control. We had no idea of the challenge yet to come.

Stress is Relative!

Artwork by Tewa Pueblo artist Betty Tsosie

CHAPTER 13

Hello New Mexico!

The girls and I never saw the New Mexico mountains in the distance as we traveled westward since it was well after dark as I crossed into the state. My first visual cue of the landscape around Albuquerque was the sight of high rock walls lining the highway through Tijeras canyon.

Speeding through the darkness I rounded a curve and looked down over a glorious basin of glowing lights spilling out across the Rio Grande valley. A crystal clear night made it hard to see where the city lights stopped and the brilliant starfield began.

One of the advantages of coming from a very large family is that we have relatives everywhere. One of my cousins used to live in Albuquerque and she had a friend who offered us a place to stay until we found an apartment.

Descending into the city I quickly found my destination and put the girls and myself to bed. The next morning was the first time I truly saw the beautiful, magical place I would call home.

I pulled back the curtains and stared at jagged walls of stone reaching skyward. Sandia Mountain lay majestically across the eastern side of the city.

In awe I gazed at it – a mountain! Not some picture postcard of a distant mountain in a pastoral setting but a huge, rugged, glorious rocky mountain – right here. Up close and magnificent.

Stress is Relative!

From that moment to this, seeing Sandia Peak lifts my heart. Its name means "watermelon", it is roughly long and even on top like a watermelon on its side, but the name is most appropriate at sunset when the last long rays of golden sunlight strike the red granite which makes up most of the mountain and the hot pink glow washes over the eastern sky.

To the west of the city are seven dormant volcano cones and running north/south between these two ancient land forms is the legendary Rio Grande River. The desert sky is a clear shade of blue you never see at lower altitudes.

* * * * *

My exciting initial introduction to the cultures around me began when I took the kids to McDonald's restaurant. As I walked in there was a table to my left where a Native American family was eating. The father, mother and both son and daughter had waist long black hair – something I had never seen in conservative Indiana on men!

The second surprise came two minutes later when I ordered a Big Mac and the girl at the counter asked "with or without green chili?"

Nowadays I am addicted to the hot, flavorful green chili peppers New Mexico is famous for, but at that time it was a shock.

* * * * *

I had done some research on apartment complexes in the area while still in Oklahoma, and our first order of business was to inspect one which looked interesting and was close to where I would work. Since they had a vacant two bedroom apartment available, I signed the paperwork and we moved in the same day – with just our suitcases and ourselves.

A quick trip to Wal-Mart and we had sleeping bags and pillows to sleep in that night. The next day we visited a furniture store and arranged for the delivery of beds and a few other pieces of essential furniture, though over the next few weekends we canvassed area garage sales for most things.

After lunch the girls and I found where the Air Traffic Control Center was located – I would not go in until Monday, but this helped me get oriented. Driving around the northeast area of Albuquerque gave us a feel for the new and different environment we would be navigating. Where residential Indianapolis had large yards with few fences between homes, Albuquerque houses had really small yards surrounded mostly by stone walls at least 6 feet high!

Later I discovered that fences are important in the desert where strong spring winds blow massive amounts of sand and tumbleweeds across open land.

Luckily the classmate whose wife did babysitting for me at the Academy was living in the same apartment complex, and she readily agreed to watch the girls after school. The logistics of my life were easily dealt with.

And so I began a new phase of life.

* * * * *

Did I miss my family? Of course, but with technology leaps I could talk to them on the phone every day if I needed to. A visit home was a few hours by aircraft or a 20 hour drive down the interstate.

Did I miss doing theater? Yes, but I helped out backstage in local amateur groups in Albuquerque. I couldn't really be onstage working rotating shifts. To satisfy my artistic urges I began shooting photographs of the magnificent desert sunsets and mountains.

I am over sixty years old now and as I look back at my life it seems that I have been very lucky in so many ways. I had the courage to take an unusual path in life and it was the way that life wanted me to go, things fell into place easily.

Stress is Relative!

Like floating downstream in an inner tube, when I fought against the flow I might make it to where I thought I wanted to be, but the results were never what I really wanted to have happen. When I listened to my inner self and made decisions based on that stream of consciousness, I would find that the river was flowing exactly where I needed to be.

Taking up the challenge of a totally new career and winning my way through the Academy was really just the first step. It was not always smooth sailing. I dealt with a lot of prejudices over the next few years, but I met some great people as well.

Lesson Learned: When life steers you down a new pathway, find the fun and beauty in it.

Stress is Relative!

The stark beauty of xeriscape provided a dramatic change of environment to a girl from Indiana!

Stress is Relative!

Yucca in Bloom next to the ARTCC Microwave Towers

CHAPTER 14

Albuquerque Air Route Traffic Control Center

It was now November of 1983. The Albuquerque ARTCC was on the far north side of the city easily accessible from Highway I-25. Surrounded on three sides by raw desert there was only a small trailer park just to the south.

The facility was mainly a large brick building with tall microwave towers rising up on the south side. There were a few small outbuildings. A chain link fence surrounded the property and a small guard house and gate were out front.

After 9/11 security would be beefed up and access made more difficult, but on my first morning the guard at the front gate checked my name against a list, looked at my driver's license and pointed out the door I was to enter.

Once again, I was surrounded by those who had graduated with me from the Academy. This time I was the only female. We all met in the front lobby and were given a tour of the building by the staff training manager. The first day was all in processing, but we were shown to our classroom on the 2nd floor, where we would be spending the first few weeks.

Stress is Relative!

A glass enclosed corridor overlooked the operations floor. Operations was the size of a football field underground. Two wide aisles went from north to south with radar scopes and equipment lining each side. Ceilings were at least thirty feet high – no windows. We were told it was supposed to be bomb proof. There was low lighting overall to make reading the radar easier, with small lights over the printers and positions where controllers needed to read the flight strips.

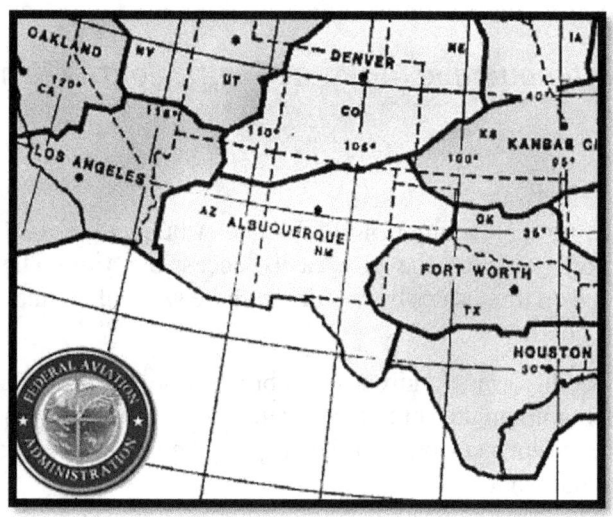

Picture of ZAB Airspace
(Albuquerque ARTCC)

Albuquerque Center covers Arizona, New Mexico and part of west Texas. The airspace is divided both laterally and horizontally into sectors.

Low altitude sectors extend from the surface to generally 18,000 feet. This is the layer of airspace where most small aircraft travel, and which

Stress is Relative!

the jets must transition through to reach the upper altitudes they were designed for. Below 18,000 some aircraft are identified on radar and talking to Air Traffic Control, but many are flying "VFR" or Visual Flight Rules. These aircraft have to abide by rules as well, and still must talk to ATC if they entered airspace governed by an ATC facility, but there is a lot of unrestricted airspace they can transit like a Jeep over open plains without having to stay on airways.

Above 18,000 feet all aircraft must be under "positive control". These aircraft measure their speed in MACH numbers – just under the speed of sound. Air Carriers, executive jets, and military aircraft going 8 miles a minute cannot see aircraft coming at them at the same speed – so controllers on the ground use the radar to identify airborne targets and their rate of closure.

The sectors were grouped into "specialties". I was assigned to the East specialty – those sectors covered the Texas panhandle and eastern New Mexico. Each specialty had a desk in the middle of the aisle where a supervisor could easily look up to see if anyone needed help. About forty controllers, six assistants and at least seven supervisors were assigned to each specialty. All told there were over 300 people actively working in operations plus support staff elsewhere in the facility during the day.

At the north end of the room an administrative area housed Area Managers, the military liaison, and weather service specialists. There are a lot of military bases and operating areas in the center. Recently the FAA had instituted a service called "Flow Control" to regulate and even out the numbers of aircraft going into and out of the larger airports – especially those which the airlines used as hubs. Two radar positions were detailed to that function.

The basement housed most of the technology and equipment including a large room dedicated to the IBM 9020 computer.

Stress is Relative!

The IBM-9020 computer at ZAB took up a whole room. In 1984 I gave a tour of the facility to a friend who was a computer geek. His excited comment was "Wow! A '9020' in WORKING CONDITION!"

The Center also had locker rooms for both men and women – though the women's was much smaller. There were break rooms with televisions and couches. A large cafeteria was open from 6am to 10pm to cover most of the 24-hour shifts. One thing it always had warm and ready was a large pot full of green chili sauce.

* * * * *

In our classroom we each had a small table with a name card on the front so the instructor could put names to faces. Dan was a genial sort of guy. The progression of our careers, he told us, would be in stages. First,

Stress is Relative!

we would spend time in the classroom memorizing the Albuquerque Center airspace – which was 100% more complicated than the map we memorized for the Academy's mythical Aero Center! Most of our time would be spent studying with some class instruction and tests.

After a couple weeks we would be taken to our specialties and an on-the-job training (OJT) instructor would be assigned to show us the ropes as Air Traffic Assistants. After a couple months as assistants we would go back into training to become D-Side controllers.

D-side means Data – this person would be using the information on the strips to keep a "picture" of where the aircraft were and doing all the intra-facility coordination. If for any reason the radar went down the D-side would take over as primary controller.

Before we began we would once again undergo non-radar graded simulations in the lab, this time the problems were specific to the areas we would actually be working. If we passed the simulations we would go out on position and work the D-Side with an OJT behind us.

We were to get "checked out" or certified, one sector at a time. Whenever we got certified on at least two sectors we would go back to the Academy for our initial radar training, then back to Albuquerque for more OJT; Position by position, sector by sector…all with someone looking over your shoulder.

At fixed points in the training the FAA would increase our salaries. These benchmarks also came with other benefits. If a person reached a certain level, but failed to attain the next level, they might terminated your employment or may offer the option of transferring to a different Air Traffic Control facility, one where certification levels already achieved qualified you to work.

* * * * *

Stress is Relative!

During the first few weeks in the classroom when I was re-united with my Academy classmates I discovered that several of them were more resistant to women in the workforce than I originally thought.

The second day of class I met one of the few women controllers working at the Center. Nancy was a delightful lady who introduced me to the Professional Women Controllers Association. PWC was a national non-profit group whose purpose was to offer emotional support for those who, like me, found themselves in a job where women were scarce.

I set the small brochure about PWC on my desk. One of the guys who had been in the sister class at the academy, Duffy, came by and seeing on my desk began cussing at a low level, then sneeringly said to me "What do you need that shit for?" Surprised, I responded "I think it's because of attitudes like yours!"

At one point there was a short conversation among some of the guys who did believe that men and women had different responsibilities. I remember Ted said, "I have never had a women open a door for me!"

Usually at the end of the day we would all trot out en masse to the parking lot. That day I was the first to the door and held it open as the guys barreled through. Ted passed me, then stopped and turned around saying "That doesn't count!"

* * * * *

The next day in the middle of class, Rod was called out by the instructor for a meeting. When he came back in he told us he was being removed from training. He said something had come up with his vision which medically disqualified for Center or Tower work. However, the FAA was reassigning him to the third division of Air Traffic – Flight Service.

Rod said goodbye to everyone. He went back to the Academy for another four months, then moved to Kankakee Flight Service in Illinois, where he spent most of his career.

Stress is Relative!

Once our tasks were laid out for us and the schedule known, our days were mostly spent in study – with no instructor in the room. Some of the young men in our group took advantage of this to discuss their investigation into the seedier side of life in Albuquerque - like the strip joints and where they got drunk last night. Tony was a small guy with a big ego, always bragging about his most recent conquest.

One morning we were studying on our own for a couple hours when Tony stood up and stretched, then announced he was going to "take a leak". He said, "Hey, Rose, you wanna come along and hold it for me?"

I turned and looked at him, and without saying a word I walked out of the room and closed the door. Listening for a minute I heard the other guys telling Tony that I was probably going to HR and if he didn't want to get fired he better find me and apologize quickly.

I went into the Ladies room and thought for a few minutes. He'd really disgusted me. I did not want to make waves, all I wanted was a fair chance of making the grade. Most certainly I did not want to get anyone fired, but I did not want Tony thinking he could harass me like that either. I decided to see what he would do.

As I walked back to my desk I noted Tony was not in the room. The others quietly glanced up at me then turned their attention to their maps. I sat down and studied mine. When Tony came back in he came by and in a cajoling tone said, "Hey, Rose, you know I was just kidding, right?"

Not looking at him, I simply said, "It was NOT funny." The room was quiet as he went back to his seat.

He never gave me any more guff after that.

* * * * *

You know how you always think of a good come back line well after someone has been that annoying? You always wish you'd said something brilliantly pointed?

Stress is Relative!

To this day, when he asked me if I wanted to come along and "hold it" I wish I would have responded with "Sorry, Tony, I didn't bring my tweezers today."

* * * * *

The FAA had specific numbers of hours they allow for various levels of training. Frequently, we were left alone to study and by the afternoon the group would get bored with drawing the maps and memorizing frequencies.

Suddenly out of nowhere paper balls or rubber bands would bop you. Sometimes it escalated so everyone participated.

One of my classmates, a nice fellow named Stef who came from Ohio, had enthusiastically discovered the fiery flavor of green chile. He sat at the desk in front of me and he loved to slather the green chile sauce from the cafeteria on his breakfast huevos rancheros, on his luncheon carne adovada burrito and everything else he ate.

Unfortunately it seemed to give him some really offensive flatulence. I started bringing cans of Lysol spray to work and setting them on my desk.

One day he let out with a really loud ripsnorter of a fart. EVERYONE in the room stood up and moved to the opposite wall – as if it had been rehearsed. We all stood there and stared at him.

Stef said, "What?! If I try to hold it in, it hurts!"

CHAPTER 15

On the Job Training

At the end of classroom training after the last test we were taken down to our specialties and introduced to the supervisors and controllers on duty. Starting the next day, we would be working rotating shifts – evenings, days and a midnight each week. Our weekends would be assigned to us. I drew Tuesday/Wednesday. That was tough for a single Mom, but I was able to strike a deal with one of my classmate's wives.

The fact that training did not always end in success was brought home to me when Luke, Dean and I were being introduced to the men on duty in the East specialty.

One of them was slunk back in his chair chewing on a toothpick and watching the radar casually. Not glancing up he said "Until you're checked out I don't wanna know your name."

Some of the controllers were very helpful, others had a scornful attitude, and still others were just passive as far as trainees were concerned. One thing I noted was that there was a plethora of "characters" in the group.

There was one guy, OJ, who was about 45 and worked out every day. He would call everyone "Weenie". He preferred to plaster himself to the radar and work the busy times, but during the slack times he would get up and joke with guys then challenge them to see who could do the most push-ups – one handed.

Stress is Relative!

My supervisor, Buck, was a former Marine master sergeant, and he looked like he ate rocks for breakfast – maybe with jalapenos on top. The supervisors were required to stay proficient working on position in operations several days a month. When Buck was working radar he would glue himself to a position for four to five hours without a break – leading by example. He bragged that he'd been working for thirty years and had never taken a day of sick leave.

* * * * *

Flight Strips display the aircraft's flight plan information

Charlie, my A-side instructor, was 6' 5" inches tall. Since I am only 5'3" he looked like a Great Dane towering over a Corgi. He had a great sense of humor. He'd casually walk over to where I was standing, set his elbow on my head and ask, "Anybody see Rose?"

Being an assistant controller, or A-side, was really easy. The printer would spit out flight strips for aircraft thirty minutes prior to their entering our airspace. An assistant would tear off the strip, stuff it in a strip holder and place it in the "pending" bay at the appropriate sector. Sometimes the computer would send several strips on the same aircraft – but the

Stress is Relative!

controllers only wanted or needed one, so we had to know which contained the most pertinent information.

On a daily basis there were known times of dense traffic where every sector would have both a Radar (R-Side) and a manual (D-Side) controller working the positions. When traffic slacked off the two controllers assigned would spell each other for breaks if they were both qualified, with one person handling both responsibilities.

The supervisor made sure everyone had breaks and lunch time slots. If traffic was particularly dense the supervisor would plug in behind the R-Side and watch the activity – providing another pair of eyes.

When things were slack in the evenings some of the sectors would be combined – the radar was reconfigured to cover more than one area or set of altitudes. Usually all the sectors in a given Specialty were combined during a midnight shift.

The Amarillo Low sector controller would expand the radar to cover all the other sectors in the East Specialty area – both high and low altitude. During the midnight shift the controller in that area monitored traffic from 70 miles northeast of Amarillo, south to the big bend area of Texas, west to El Paso, then North to Cimarron, New Mexico and back around to the Texas panhandle.

I accidentally discovered one of the old misogynistic holdouts of a male dominated environment one evening as I glanced over my shoulder towards the Amarillo Low sector. Over every radar scope was a map of the sector that controllers could glance at for quick reference if needed. On an evening shift I once saw one of the guys pull the map panel out to peek at what was behind it. That is when I saw the picture of a naked woman hidden there.

The FAA's training system was largely subjective. Early on we realized that if the controllers liked you it was reflected in the training records. The OJT (on-the-job-training) controllers received 5% over base salary to train you because if you screw up they have to take the heat. Every day the OJT sits behind you with a clipboard and writes down anything he thinks needs to be worked on.

Stress is Relative!

Each time you began a new sector the instructor would start out writing up a long list of things they want to discuss with you at the end of the shift. As your performance improved the list would normally get shorter and dwindle to nothing just before you are given a check ride by the supervisor.

How much they put on the list is highly subjective.

For the most part I did not perceive any particular dislike from the people I worked with based on gender – it seemed that most of the Full-Performance-Level (FPL) controllers were equally distrustful of all trainees.

There was only one woman who was an FPL in my specialty, and across the facility at the time I only remember 6 women out of nearly 300 controllers who were FPLs.

Like I said before, it wasn't a career most girls even knew about as a career option back then.

* * * * *

I checked out on the Assistant duties easily and became accustomed to the daily rhythm of traffic, and to the various personalities I worked with. In office environments everyone usually has their own space – a desk or area that they and a few others would occupy for eight hours a day.

Each specialty in the Center contained between 8 and 10 radar sectors. These were lined up next to each other and the controllers were rotated between the sectors every day. The supervisor's drew up the rotation of assignments every day, so you never knew in advance who you would be working a sector with.

The majority of controllers are "A" type personalities. I sometimes felt sorry for the supervisors having to ride herd on that group.

After doctors and pilots, controllers supposedly have the highest divorce rate. It is easy to understand why. There was one supervisor in

Stress is Relative!

the North specialty whose love life provided amusement for everyone. He was on his fifth wife.

These guys are trained to *know* that whatever they do is right – it has to be. They have to know that their decisions are correct and that the pilots will obey any instructions given, which breeds an inflated ego. That kind of daily input tends to carry over to your home life. Mates tend to be annoyed by that trait over time.

Mind you, this is a stereotype, not all the guys were like that. One of the controllers in the North Specialty, Wayne, was a truly generous soul. He loved astronomy and photography. He was a gifted amateur photographer and had a fully equipped darkroom in his garage.

My classmate, Dean and I were both interested in photography and Wayne graciously taught us how to develop color film and let us use his darkroom as long as we kept it supplied.

This was in 1984. I learned there is an ebb and flow to the pace of each sector in the Center airspace. A lot of it is driven by the airlines as they rush into their HUB airports in such a way as to load and unload passengers, minimizing their ground time.

Mornings had every position in the Center gazing intently at radars. There was the hum of voices giving control instructions, and answering calls from other sectors and ATC facilities.

This had been going on for about two hours one day, and the morning rush was beginning to die back when one controller, Skip, pushed his chair back from position and in a loud voice sang out "I'm about to LOSE CONTROL and I think I LIKE IT!" Just a momentary joke, but everyone got a chuckle out of it.

ATC is a lot like that. Sometimes you have long periods of slow traffic punctuated by short bursts of almost frenetic activity. Sometimes you are so continuously busy that you are surprised when someone taps you on the shoulder to replace you and several hours have gone by!

Stress is Relative!

CHAPTER 16

D-Side Simulations

We worked out in Operations until after the holidays that year, then went back into training. This time we had little time in the classroom before we began non-radar simulation testing again down in a small cramped simulation room in the basement of the building.

The set up was different from the Academy in that only two people were tested at a time, and they were each working problems specific to the specialty they were assigned. Those of us who were not being tested took turns acting as remote pilots and other controllers with which the trainee had to communicate. This made for a very interesting situation because the remotes were able to tell what errors the trainee being tested made while the simulation was in progress.

We noted that instructors grading the exams sometimes did not catch all the errors made. When our classmates came out everyone compared notes. Most of the things missed would be small phraseology errors or an occasional procedural error.

This time we had to pass every simulation. The simulations were progressively more complicated and if you failed one you were allowed to try another at the same level. If you failed at that level again, you were immediately dismissed from the program.

I passed the first four graded problems. During the fifth one the evaluator, Mike, gave me a separation error – an automatic failure. As we went over it together though he discovered he'd heard me wrong and reversed the score.

As I went back into the classroom the two who had been my remotes were asking about the outcome. One of them was the guy who had been snide about the PWC brochure on my desk, Duffy. I told them that the evaluator thought I had had a separation error, but then we discovered it was done correctly.

The two of them however had noticed that I had given a radial one degree short of the mandatory fifteen to a different aircraft which was another type of separation error. I'd probably done it while the evaluator was writing down what he thought was an error.

Half an hour later the evaluator cornered me alone in a hallway

"I understand that I missed one on you.... I'll be watching you like a hawk from now on."

Duffy, who had failed his problem and was now on probation until his next test, had done what none of the rest of us had done...he'd run down to the instructors and ratted me out.

Duffy passed his make-up problem and continued training for another week. Then he failed another one and the make-up to that one. Since he'd progressed to that level of training he was allowed to stay on as an assistant until he could be sent to an FAA facility back east with less traffic where he might be able to achieve certification.

We lost three from our class during the simulations. I passed the rest of mine and went on to the next phase of training on the Operations Floor.

Stress is Relative!

Stress is Relative!

CHAPTER 17

D-Side (Manual or Data control) OJT

Once we got back to operations we began working the D-side, or Manual Control position. Whoever is working D-Side keeps a mental picture of where aircraft are by constantly perusing the Data strips. If for any reason the radar goes down, the D-Side controller is supposed to have the picture in his mind clear enough to take over controlling the aircraft in his sector.

On a daily basis, there is always someone working the radar position, with light to moderate traffic one person can keep track of both responsibilities. The D-side is manned during times of higher more intense traffic.

The Manual Controller organizes the strips in the bays and coordinates activities with other air traffic facilities while the Radar R-Side controller is the one talking to the aircraft. D-Side watches what the Radar guy is doing and learns to anticipate what actions need to be taken.

As trainees we began working the D-Side during light traffic initially and as our skill progressed we would be assigned during higher traffic periods. Every so often the supervisor is required to evaluate your progress. These are referred to check rides

This is where the hours of memorizing frequencies and dial codes paid off. You didn't have time to take out the books and charts to see what

Stress is Relative!

button operated the direct line to a specific Tower and what two digit dial code reached a specific control position within the tower – you just had to know it!

* * * * *

In addition to official check rides the supervisor might sit with you just to see how things were coming. Buck was looking over my shoulder one day early in my training. I called Roswell Approach with some information – the strip in my hand showed the aircraft call sign as VM3G135 – Marine 3Golf135.

The identifier for Navy is VV. As I glanced at the strip I inadvertently said "Navy" rather than Marine, then went to correct myself, but not before a loud bang caused me to jump straight up and turn around. My supervisor had just slammed the clipboard on the back of the chair behind me.

"NEVER call a Marine, NAVY!" He barked then glared at me.

Oops...Did I mention that Buck was a former Marine Master Sergeant?

I didn't do that again!

CHAPTER 18

Fam Flights

At a specific point in our training we became eligible to take Familiarization Flights or "FAM Flights" with the airlines, private pilots, or other flying organizations. During the flight, Controllers are supposed to sit in the cockpit of the aircraft. These flights are meant to be educational in nature – allowing Controllers to observe cockpit procedures and equipment.

To request a FAM flight specialists chose the flights they want to take (which usually just happen to coincide with vacation plans) and submitted the paperwork to the supervisor to pass up to the facility manager. They sent it to the airlines for their approval. Once approved, we showed up at the airport at the appropriate time and checked in with the airline's operations office.

It did not automatically follow that we got to hop on the plane at that point. There were others who may get priority to use the "Jumpseat" on the flight we chose. If an official FAA inspector was doing an evaluation on the flight he receives first priority. After him, any pilot working for the airline who wanted to travel on the aircraft could claim the seat – though if there were any empty seats in the main cabin he could choose to ride there.

Stress is Relative!

So it could be hit or miss as to whether you got your first choice of flight, but the airlines were very cooperative overall.

The first time I did this I purchased tickets for my daughters on the same flights I was planning to fly in the cockpit. They were about eight and nine years old at the time.

I was flying with Delta Airlines and they were very accommodating. My daughters were seated halfway back in the aircraft, but I was able to get them settled in before taking my place in the cockpit.

A flight attendant came in to see me after all the passengers had been seated and told me that since there were two empty seats in First Class, they'd decided to move the girls up closer to the cockpit. I came out to check on them a couple times. They were having a ball.

* * * * *

I miss flying in the jump seat. Seeing expansive horizons, circular rainbows, glorious sunsets, and blankets of stars from the cockpit beat the heck out of scrunching down and looking through a passenger window. You could watch the instruments and listen to ATC and best of all you could just TALK to the pilots rather than ordering them around the way I did at work.

Some of the pilots were very adamant that FAM flights were for training, not just freeloading a ride – so they trained me. I learned how to open and close the doors on the aircraft, and how to open the cockpit window to toss out a knotted rope you could climb down in case of an emergency landing. Several pilots went over how all the instruments worked and gave me insights as to the differences between the types of aircraft.

In most airlines, the jump seat is a small shelf with a cushion which folds down from the wall behind the pilot. It had seat belts that came down over the shoulders, and across your lap. Some seats had one extra that came up from under the seat. They all attached to a large clasp at your waist.

Stress is Relative!

Donning the big black oxygen mask always made a mess out of my hair, but it had to be adjusted and set aside just in case. Headphones were set so that you covered one ear to hear ATC and left the other one free to hear what was going on around you.

I learned such tidbits as Boeing 727's climb slowly but drop quickly – so if ATC has to change a B727's altitude, it's better to descend him. On the other hand, Boeing 737's like to climb. Learjet pilots love unrestricted climbs on departure. One pilot told me a Lear is the next best thing to flying a fighter plane.

Flying with friends in their small aircraft is an AWESOME experience!

Stress is Relative!

FAM flights weren't just about getting free rides in air carriers. I've flown with a lot of private pilots in small aircraft – those are a lot of fun!

Some of the more unusual flights I participated in included a ride in a National Guard UH60 helicopter as it practiced rescue maneuvers in the mountains, and a NASA trainer doing shuttle landing practice.

* * * * *

On a long trip from Seattle to Anchorage I was with a pair of older male pilots who grudgingly let me fly in their cockpit. They had stuck pictures of women with their legs spread in the light recesses of the ceiling instrument panel.

I did not say a word about seeing those pictures, but I am sure they were just waiting for me to do so. They did not offer me any other form of disrespect. Hey, I was getting a free ride to Alaska, I could be blind for 4 hours.

The vast majority of the pilots I have ridden with were great. I knew things were beginning to change when I was on a Delta flight with a female co-pilot. One of the last air carrier trips I took had females in both the Captain and co-pilot seats!

Over the past 34 years I figure I've ridden in 24 different kinds of aircraft – helicopters, jets, little Cessna trainers, and hot air balloons. Next year I've determined I'll take up my friend Jon's offer and go for a ride in his glider.

After I retired I took a trip to visit family. I sat down in my airline seat next to the tiny window. Thinking of the FAM flights I'd taken over the years I thought to myself how much I would prefer to be flying in the uncomfortable little bitty jump seat again – even if I had to pay for the privilege.

* * * * *

Stress is Relative!

During our training at the ARTCC, if we were perceived as doing well, some controllers would allow trainees to do the Radar controlling while listening to every word on the midnight shift when there were very few active flights– we called it bootleg time.

Part of being in operations is a need to keep track of who is performing what duties and who you are talking to over the communications or "com" lines. Early on we were assigned a set of initials that were unique to each person in the facility. When there are hundreds of people working in a place you are going to have a lot of them with the same initials, so in order to identify who is who there is a master list you can choose from. At the end of every communication between ATC facilities the controllers must sign off with those initials.

At the time my married surname began with a D, so normally I would have been RD, but that set of initials was taken. So was RK – my maiden name initials. With over 300 people in that building the pickings were slim, so I ended up with QD. It wasn't until later that I found out the downside of that decision.

I was getting some bootleg time on a midnight shift. Talking to Amarillo Tower I signed off "QD" – which said quickly sounds like "Cutie". The Tower controller came back with "I'll bet you are!"

It seems whatever initials a woman has the guys try to make something out of it. One lady in another specialty had the initials BJ – which were her real initials. I'd hear the more juvenile personalities of the facility snicker and call her "Blow Job".

* * * * *

Whenever someone completed their training and became an FPL (Full Performance Level) controller it was customary for them to have a check-out party and invite everyone in the specialty. One of the students ahead of our class, Bruce, was having a party at his place.

I showed up about sunset and the party was already in full swing. A lot of people and their families were there. As I walked into the house the kitchen to the left was full of guys chanting someone's name, then

Stress is Relative!

cheering. They would pick on one of their number and yell their name loudly until they drank a shot of whiskey.

Unfortunately, one of them saw me. Loudly I heard "ROSE ROSE ROSE ROSE," and someone pulled me out of the hallway into the kitchen and one of the supervisors – Roger- slapped a shot glass in my hand.

I had a dilemma. I can't drink alcohol. Like a lot of people, I gave it a try back in college, but even one sip sends me retching. But here I was with all the guys wanting me to participate in their little game. Trying to be a good sport I knocked it back, they cheered and let me go.

The bathroom was taken so I went outside and threw up out on the front lawn. When I went back in I ran into Roger and told him that I wasn't feeling well and please do not do that to me again.

Many of the controller's wives knew each other and were gathered around the large dining table talking. Others were scattered around the house in the Den and backyard.

I was playing a board game with one of the kids an hour later when I heard "ROSE ROSE ROSE ROSE" coming from the other end of the house. I was seated on the floor when a couple guys came in and lifted me up and pulled me into the dining room.

Roger, himself, lifted my hand and slapped the shot glass in it.

> **The room got totally quiet.**

I was pissed. Something hot and angry inside me said *NO*. I took that shot glass and dumped it over the top of Roger's bald head then set it down hard on the table.

The room got totally quiet.

I looked at him and said flatly "I told you NOT to do that to me again." I walked out of the room and back to my game.

The shot drinking stopped after that.

Stress is Relative!

* * * * *

At work the next day a few of the people came up and quietly told me they wished they had the courage to do that. I have to give Roger credit, he came up and apologized in public.

* * * * *

I had a problem retaining primary OJT instructors. The first one was with me for a week and then got promoted to a staff job. The second one was with me for another week then received a desired transfer to another Center. The third one trained me for two weeks when he won a supervisory job.

Apparently it was a great career move to be sitting with me…but it made training a lot more difficult because every person has different techniques to handle different situations and they all think their way is right. Which meant that for each new trainer came a period of adjustment to the new techniques.

They ARE right, all of them. There are a lot of options for how to handle problems. Some controllers will climb or descend an aircraft, some will turn them in toward the other aircraft knowing that the first aircraft won't be there by the time the second one gets there.

As a trainee I was glad to know my options but frustrated that each time I got a new OJT they would fill up the page with things they perceived we needed to discuss until they learned to trust me. Finally I got Matthew as my OJT. Matt was tough, but fair.

When I did something he felt could be done better he explained why and he offered encouragement and compliments instead of just constant criticism.

* * * * *

Stress is Relative!

I checked out on a few of my D-Side positions and was told that they had a slot for me in Radar training at the Academy in Oklahoma City.

After a short three weeks I came back to the Center and resumed accumulating D-Side sectors, but was given more bootleg time during midshifts from some of the controllers who were looking at me with a bit more respect.

Unfortunately for me, my instructor, Matt, got a promotion shortly thereafter.

CHAPTER 19

Something Is Out of Whack

It was almost two years after I had begun my journey in ATC when I started having some problems physically. For no reason it seemed I was suddenly gaining weight and feeling very lethargic. My face sprouted zits – something that I had not endured since high school.

There were other symptoms as well. For instance, I might just be chatting with someone amicably and suddenly I had tears flowing down my face! I wasn't upset about anything, they were just there!

My primary care doctor had me tested for diabetes and a few other things – but that was not it so he made an appointment with an endocrinologist.

* * * * *

The day before I was to see the specialist Buck called me back into the supervisor's office and gave me a royal dressing down.

"What's going on? Why are you working the most difficult traffic with no problems in the morning but making stupid piddly little errors during the slow times!"

Explanations about what had been happening and that I was going to see a doctor about it began to tumble from my mouth, but my former-marine never-been-sick-a-day-in-his-life supervisor looked at me and said

Stress is Relative!

"Lady, there is nothing wrong with you…YOU just can't handle the stress of training."

I left that day not knowing what in the world was happening to me. Was he right? Was it job stress causing all of this? What would I do if it was? Everything had been going so well up to that point.

* * * * *

I will always look back on my trip to the Endocrinologist with gratitude. Dr. Neil Friedman listened carefully to everything I said then had me get undressed. His nurse took notes as he looked me over carefully and minutely from top to toe externally and internally as well. I was on his examining table for more than an hour.

Afterwards he had me get dressed and meet him in his office.

"First of all," he said, "You are not crazy, there is something badly wrong with you."

I think those are the most blessed words I had ever heard! I wasn't crazy, I wasn't just stressing over training. Yeah, there was something wrong, but it was something DEFINABLY wrong – it wasn't just something in my head.

> **I Was NOT Crazy!**

He went on to tell me that in addition to the pimples I had on my face, back and shoulders he noted I was losing hair at my temples, and my female organs were enlarged. My left ovary was the size of a grapefruit and the right one was the size of a baseball.

He knew it had to do with the hormonal balance in my system but we would have to do a lot of tests to determine exactly which hormones were the problem. For the next two months I would go in and get 6 to 8 big vials of blood drawn every two weeks until they isolated what was wonky.

He gave me a note which I took to work. My supervisor gave it to the flight surgeon who worked full time at the Center. Dr. Gray immediately rescinded my medical clearance – I was out of training.

Stress is Relative!

Because I was not sick enough to have to stay in bed all the time I continued working – but just as an A-side assistant. I was still useful but this task does not require a person to be as mentally focused. For the next few months I came in to work and sat at a printer and carefully loaded and delivered the strips and did little else. This was a blessing because to be honest I had no energy.

After about two months they isolated the problem. I had severe polycystic ovary disease. Little cysts covered my ovaries and they were attacking my eggs. Every person carries both several kinds of male hormones and female hormones in their systems. The eggs put out estrogen in a woman's body – so two of the male hormones in my system were building up without the countering chemical causing me to be in a world of hurt both physically and emotionally.

The doctor put me on a regimen of hormonal medications that over time would create a balance, but he told me it would probably be another eight months before I was back to normal.

However, back at work, as soon as they identified the problem and put me on medication the flight surgeon recertified me for training!

Women's medical issues at that time were not considered disqualifying no matter the toll they took on a person. It has changed considerably since then.

It had been months since I was medically decertified and I was not ready to resume training – the effects of the imbalance still caused me to be lethargic. The FAA only authorizes a limited number of hours for training. I had used most of them while the illness was creeping up on me and some of that time was burnt each time I was assigned a new OJT instructor. That plus the months of no training and the fact that I was still not feeling well pretty much nailed me.

* * * * *

Ever since childhood I've had vivid dreams, full of emotion, feeling and color. Back in Indiana I'd once had a conversation with a friend who

Stress is Relative!

was a psychologist about them. He told me that dreams are a vector through which the subconscious communicates with the conscious mind.

During this phase of my training where my future seemed bleak I had a dream where I was flying a small aircraft through a beautiful blue sky over rolling green hills. Suddenly out of nowhere a black jet zoomed up and began shooting at me. I tried to zigzag away but it was much too fast and maneuverable.

Suddenly I found myself standing on the ground looking into a ravine. My aircraft was a jumble of wreckage at the bottom of the ravine.

My dream-self looked upon it sadly but then I realized that I was alive and standing in a beautiful field on a lovely day. I woke with renewed hope and a realization that whatever happened things would turn out well.

* * * * *

At work I was told that since I had not checked out within the FAA's allotted time period I was to be washed out.

The good news was that I had reached a plateau in my training that would allow me to directly transfer to a lower traffic level Air Traffic Control Tower. The Center training manager found two towers in need of controllers and the managers indicated they wanted me – one was in Houma, Louisiana – outside of New Orleans, and one was in Pontiac, Michigan. I opted for Michigan and went back home to begin packing.

My daughters liked that Pontiac was only a couple hours north of Indianapolis, so we'd be able to see our extended family more often. We put our house up on the market and I continued to work as an air traffic assistant while waiting for my orders to appear.

Surprisingly our house sold the first day it was listed, and I had no transfer paperwork yet. Thinking we would only be there a short while, I signed a month to month lease at an apartment complex and moved out.

Then the U.S. Congress fouled up our plans.

Stress is Relative!

    I came in to work and was called to the training manager's office. Congress had just passed what was titled the Graham-Rudman Bill after the two who sponsored it. This bill called a halt to ALL government employee relocations for at least six months. They were trying to balance the budget.

    This meant no tower job – I offered to pay my own way but that was not allowed. The Center kept me on as an A-Side for a few months, then a Clearance Delivery/Flight Data specialist job opened up with the ATC Tower at Albuquerque International airport. Since there was no "move" involved, I was allowed to transition to the Tower, but only as an assistant – not a trainee.

Stress is Relative!

Albuquerque Air Traffic Control Tower

Circa 1987

Stress is Relative!

CHAPTER 20

Becoming a Tower Flower

ABQ ATCT (Albuquerque Air Traffic Control Tower)

The Albuquerque International Airport – also called the Sunport – is located on the far south side of Albuquerque; an easy segue from Interstate 25. I began working there immediately with very little training as my ARTCC job function had already given me the basics and was far more advanced than the work I was to do in the Tower.

I was not on the training track to become a full performance level controller (FPL), but that was just fine. The two positions I would be working were Clearance Delivery and Flight Data. These responsibilities were similar to what I'd been doing at the Center, they were easy, and I was still recovering.

Accustomed to being a very high energy person, I found that dealing with an energy sapping physical condition made my mind feel sluggish as well. My jobs at the Tower were well within my capability. After a few months, when I started feeling like myself again, I started volunteering for extra duties. When I am at normal energy levels my "boredom threshold" is very low.

Although my stay in the tower was short – only about a year, it widened my understanding of the National Airspace System. I saw enough to realize that if I had known the difference between working in

Stress is Relative!

the tower environment and working for a Center, I might have put that down as my first choice on the FAA entrance application.

Because most people are not familiar with the lingo, I am going to digress and explain a bit about how the system works.

Albuquerque had enough traffic to rate both a Tower and an Approach Control. Tower handles aircraft departing and landing the airport surface. The Approach was located at the base of the tower – a darkened room where controllers identified departures and arrivals on Radar and kept them separated within a 30 mile radius of the airport up to 17,000 feet. Controllers at Albuquerque worked both the Tower cab and the Approach control on alternate days.

The Tower normally had at least four people on duty at any given time during the day – the Clearance Delivery/Flight Data specialist, a Ground controller, a Local controller and a supervisor. During busy periods there might be a person manning the Coordinator position to back up Local Control.

At night the positions combined as traffic decreased so that only one person could handle all those duties after midnight.

Generally speaking, after a pilot does his preflight briefing and files a flight plan (more on that later), he calls the Tower's Clearance Delivery radio frequency and requests a clearance.

A "clearance" is a set of instructions delineating exactly what headings and altitudes an aircraft is assigned to fly based on his flight plan request. When an aircraft is "cleared" it literally means that the controllers have ensured the airspace he is about to enter has no other aircraft in the way.

Working the Clearance Delivery (CD) position, I spoke to aircraft still parked on the ramp, ensuring the pilot knows what route he is expected to take from the time he departs the surface to whenever he either lands (IFR) or leaves controlled airspace (VFR).

Once the pilot is ready to move the aircraft, he calls Ground Control to get permission to taxi to the runway. Ground Control monitors and

Stress is Relative!

controls the movement of aircraft and all other vehicles rolling around the airport surface. The only surface area he does not control is the Runway.

When the aircraft has reached the end of the runway he switches to the Local Control frequency (which is the only one the pilot's call "Tower" on radio). Local Control tells him when to taxi onto the runway.

The Local controller is continuously scanning the sky for inbound traffic. He "clears" aircraft to land or depart from a given runway. He has information strips on both the inbound and outbound aircraft. During busy periods the Coordinator will do the strip marking and distribution while Local talks to the aircraft and continuously scans the surrounding skies.

Once the aircraft departs the surface he is instructed to contact Approach and the paper strip containing the data on the aircraft was affixed to a plastic holder and dropped down a very long tube to the Radar room at the base of the tower.

. The Approach Control room contained four large radar screens. The room is always kept dark with small desk lamps lighting the flight data area and supervisory desks. During busy times all the radar scopes would be occupied with controllers working the aircraft in the 4 quadrants around the airport. Between rushes, the sectors would combine to two during the day, and one in the evening.

Once a departing aircraft reaches the outer limits of the Approach airspace, it is either handed off to the ARTCC if it is IFR aircraft or if it is flying VFR Radar service is terminated and the aircraft goes its merry way into uncontrolled airspace.

Traffic is always dense close into the airport, so the RADAR (acronym for Radio Detection and Ranging) is located on or very near the airfield. Since the accuracy of returns is much finer close to the radar antennae, an Approach Control can run aircraft up to three miles apart at the same altitude. The ARTCC cannot let aircraft fly any closer than five miles because they are getting returns from a greater distance.

Stress is Relative!

* * * * *

The 360 degree view from the Tower made the job a delight. I could see the whole Rio Grande valley, the mountains, the city, and the west mesa all the way to the volcanos. To the south you could see as far as Socorro Mountain nearly, 80 miles away. Now I could actually see the aircraft I spoke to.

Albuquerque is a joint-use airport, meaning that it was both civilian and military. The two main runways were about two miles long so large air carriers and huge B52 bombers could use them. There were also shorter runways for smaller private aircraft to use during times when traffic density necessitated.

Sunrise and sunset from the tower is almost always glorious. Sometimes I would bring a camera to work to capture the beauty. It was a great elevation for getting pictures of various aircraft as they took off and landed.

* * * * *

I worked in the original tower at Albuquerque International, which had a double cab, on the south side of the airfield. The room at the top of the tower is the cab, the lower cab on this one was used as a break room primarily so that you didn't have to take the tiny elevator or stairs all the way down to the ground floor.

A very small toilet facility served both men and women just off the lower cab. One summer day as I was using it I noticed a small edge of paper sticking out of the cover to the controls for the small heater situated on the wall about a foot from the front of the toilet.

It was an X-Rated Hustler magazine. (sigh)

* * * * *

In aviation we keep a close watch on weather as it can become nasty in a hurry. I was in the Tower cab one day when we noticed a black haze way out west on the mesa. The winds were rising and we could

Stress is Relative!

see a dark land based cloud sweeping down into the Rio Grande Valley then upwards toward us on the east side of the city.

The sky grew darker as an enormous wall of sand and debris breached the fence west of Runway 8/26. A massive horde of tumbleweeds, some as large as Volkswagen bugs, rolled eastwards on the runway in front of an extraordinary gust front. The wind slammed into the tower…and the tower SWAAYYYED!

That was scary and the supervisor ordered everyone not actively working a position to head downstairs until the winds abated.

Another time in the tower we were surrounded by a shallow fog that was above the level of the cab. This was unusual for our desert climate, we could not see anything outside the windows. Suddenly a flight of birds burst into view – at the last second the flock split in half and went around the cab forming up again on the other side.

As the day heated up the fog lowered so that we began to see the tails of the larger jets sticking up above it as they taxied to the end of the runway like sharks in water.

* * * * *

During my many years of voice lessons and a short stint in broadcast I'd developed a fairly low rounded and slightly melodic speaking voice which carried over radio frequencies well.

One day after I'd given a clearance to a local aircraft who'd heard me several times before he said, "You have a great voice, you should be in radio!"

I chuckled and responded over the frequency – "I AM in radio, eight hours a day…and the pay is a lot better!"

* * * * *

There were a few fully rated female controllers in the tower, though I didn't really see them often on the shifts I worked.

Stress is Relative!

One of them, Angie, was from Oklahoma, and she liked to work the midnight shift. At that time only one person would work the tower from midnight to 4am. A small RADAR screen alerted them to any inbound traffic – it was easy to see at night.

Angie had an intriguing southern accent. She told me that one night an air carrier came in about 2am. Center turned the aircraft onto her frequency and she gave him his approach, landing and taxi clearances.

The co-pilot came on frequency, "Hey, Tower, the Captain wants to know what you're doing up there all alone?"

To which Angie replied truthfully. "Painting my toenails".

After a moments pause, he called again and said "The Captain wants to know if the door's locked?"

* * * * *

Pilots who fly in and out of the same airport day after day develop a slightly more relaxed rapport with the controllers on duty in the tower. Sometimes they would come up and visit, or stop by with a Christmas gift such as a box of chocolates for the people on duty.

One of them was a local rancher who owned both a large cattle ranch in northwest New Mexico as well as a pecan farm in the southeastern part of the state. Homer would stop by once a year with a large brown paper grocery bag bulging with freshly picked pecans – wonderfully delicious!

Although the pilots were not supposed to make idle chatter on the frequencies we'd occasionally have amusing comments. One day a Southwest Airlines jet was dawdling as it moved down the taxiway towards the terminal because another aircraft had yet to clear out of the gate he needed to park in. At the time Southwest stock was soaring and they were quickly becoming one of the most popular airlines in the country.

Behind him was a Delta jet with a captain wanting to get to the gate and discharge his passengers. On the Ground control frequency we heard spoken:

Stress is Relative!

"BEEP, BEEP, Get that mustard colored airplane out of my way!"

The Southwest captain responded. "We are NOT mustard colored, we are gold and orange and WE carry Texas Gold all the way to the bank!"

* * * * *

One day the commander of the New Mexico National Guard squadron located on the airfield called over to the Air Traffic Control Tower and asked if anyone wanted to go for a FAM flight in one of their UH60 helicopters. Four of us were approaching the end of our shift, so we were allowed to go.

Three women and one man climbed into a helicopter large enough to park a jeep. We took off towards the mountain chain to the east and headed up into the rocky canyons and peaks where the aircraft skimmed close to the treetops. What a ride!

The side door was left open during the flight. We appreciated the abundance of fresh air when the guy we brought started puking as the helicopter swooped along the ridgeline over the Sandia Mountains.

* * * * *

As I mentioned, Albuquerque is a joint use airport – on the west side are all the civilian facilities and the terminal, on the east side is Kirtland Air Force Base. During this period of time military ordnance was stored in Manzano base just to the east of the airport and from time to time an aircraft came in and was parked on a special pad at the base of the tower while super-secret "stuff" was being loaded.

Whenever these materials were being moved from Manzano Base to the airport the military parked tanks at all the entrances to the military base

Stress is Relative!

with their cannon pointed at the waiting lines of automobiles. Since we had to transition on to the base to get to the tower there were times when we were delayed going on duty – or able to get home!

* * * * *

One year, during the famous Albuquerque International Balloon Fiesta, the base was on lock down when strong winds pushed a balloonist south onto the base. All participants in the event are given maps showing places they are not allowed to fly, and if they see the winds are taking them the wrong direction they must land early.

This one obviously goofed. The tower stopped all aircraft departures and arrivals as it drifted towards us. It landed in the grass strip on the side of the runway and was immediately surrounded by jeeps, tanks, and lots of people with guns.

Stress is Relative!

CHAPTER 21

Trials and Tribulations

As I mentioned, once my normal energy levels came bouncing back, my job function became routine. I reached out to the manager and asked if there were other things I could do.

I began editing the facility newsletter and writing little articles for it. Later I was asked to become the supply clerk on top of my regular duties. At that time there wasn't a separate administrative secretary there to do those things.

Because I was energetic and proactive with a positive attitude I got on well with most people, but I discovered there are always people out there who dislike it whenever anyone gets what they consider "too much" attention.

One day I was called into the office of the Deputy Chief, Jerry, and was told to bring a witness. I was totally clueless as to what was going on. I brought along a friend since in my position there was no union coverage.

Jerry looked uncomfortable and started asking questions like, "Do you feel you are treated fairly here?" and "Does anyone make you feel uncomfortable?"

I said no, I like the people I worked around for the most part.

Stress is Relative!

Then he said that someone witnessed me giving someone a shoulder massage to a guy working position, was I having a relationship with anyone?

"No," I told him. I had done that for a couple people when they are were stuck working position for a long time and all tensed up.

Then he said, "We were told by someone that you are thinking about filing an EEO complaint on one of the men here…is that the case?"

I was stunned. I told him that this was not correct and asked where he heard that. He hemmed and hawed and did not answer and gave me a vague sort of indication that if I did then witnesses would say I'd given neck messages and that would be used against me.

I asked who I was supposedly going to file a complaint against and he gave the name of a supervisor who I truly liked and respected but nothing more. That is what I told him as well.

He let me go after that.

The more I thought about it the angrier I became. He called me in because of an innuendo made by someone he wouldn't name because there was a possibility that I would do something that I was legally allowed to do if in fact there was reason for it and made me feel like I had no right to do so!

A few weeks later I heard from someone else that a woman who'd been a controller for years and had the reputation of being nasty whenever others were given recognition for their work had insinuated to other controllers that I was going to do exactly what Jerry had called me in for.

Here was a woman, someone who had herself clawed her way to the top of her profession, dissing a lowly assistant just for her personal amusement.

Lesson learned: Not all MEN are prejudiced scum sucking low lives....not all WOMEN are nice people willing to help other women get ahead.

Stress is Relative!

* * * * *

Jerry apologized to me – he really wasn't a bad sort and the whole thing made him uncomfortable as well. He supported my desire to do more than just the basic job.

One day Jerry called me down to accompany him to where the FAA vehicle assigned to the tower was normally fueled. Since I wanted to help out in more ways, it had been determined that I would keep the maintenance records for it and occasionally have it serviced.

He was driving down Gibson Avenue in Albuquerque when the lady in front of us stopped unexpectedly and quickly. We were able to stop in time to keep from hitting her, but the Purolator Courier delivery van behind us did not.

The damage to our car was total, but Jerry was fine so he hopped out to see how the other driver was. As he did he called out "Now you get to find out the mountain of paperwork that goes with an accident in a government vehicle – reach in and get it out of the glove compartment for me."

I was stunned but did not think anything wrong at first – I didn't notice that the seat I was in had broken backwards. I started to lean forward to open the glove compartment, but I couldn't.

I could not move my head, my neck, or my arms above the elbow.

Jerry came bopping back, asking for the paperwork. Frozen in place I said, "Jerry," He kept talking. "Jerry....JERRY!" I CAN'T MOVE!"

Finally he realized something was wrong.

This was in the days before most people had cell phones, but he carried a radio transmit/receiver that allowed him to monitor the controllers in the tower. He called there and had the Chief come to the crash site.

Stress is Relative!

He handled the police and paperwork and I just sat there frozen. In retrospect he probably should have called for an ambulance, but I wasn't in danger of death and in no mental condition to make suggestions.

When the Chief arrived they helped me swing out to the right and stand up. I got into his car and they immediately took me to the emergency room.

As I walked in the nurse on duty looked up and saw me as I was walking in with one of them on each side and without hesitation said "Whiplash".

Sure enough, the x-rays had three vertebrae in my neck sticking out of alignment.

In the end I was on trauma leave for a month – heavy duty muscle relaxants and anti-inflammatory drugs, and full time traction. For over a year I used traction daily, decreasing the total amount little by little. Thankfully the job I was doing at the time did not require a Class A Airmen's medical certification like I had to have at Albuquerque Center.

The disks between three of my cervical vertebrae annuerised causing me to lose all the feeling in my right arm for a long time. It came back but the strength was reduced and to this day I have to make sure I sleep with my neck in just the right position or I wake up with a numb arm.

Before that time whenever I heard that someone was in traction it always sounded painful, but I can tell you that if you are really hurting, it is an incredible relief. It was the only thing that stopped a pain that would spread from my neck to my head, face, arms…everywhere. Even when I started getting better, after a day at work I would come home and head straight to the armchair where the traction was set up.

* * * * *

I had only been in the tower for a little over a year when a bid came out for the third area of Air Traffic – the Flight Service division. Since I had already gotten so far ahead in training at the Center, I had more than enough in the way of qualifications to move into that field.

CHAPTER 22

Entering Flight Service

Many of you reading may not understand what Flight Service is, or how it ties into everything. Most of the general public believes all Air Traffic Controllers work in towers – that is the only thing readily visible as they fly in and out of airports. From movies and TV they understand that radar is somehow involved as well.

In general, at the time I was going through my training there were three branches of Air Traffic Control in the government: Towers, Centers and Flight Service.

The Flight Service job deals primarily (but not exclusively) with VFR (Visual Flight Rules) and General Aviation. It is the oldest division of air traffic since it was created shortly after World War I. The duties are more diverse than either tower or center and it requires a much larger knowledge base overall. This position did require me to have a Class A Medical Certification again, luckily I passed with flying colors.

Before pilots take off, they must become familiar with all the weather and aviation related elements that are critical to each flight and Flight Service is the division that delivers the information. This includes such things as knowing which navigational aids or frequencies are out of service, the status of the runways at the destination airport or if the President of the United States has travel plans that may interfere with the trip.

Stress is Relative!

* * * * *

Flight Service people hold credentials as weather observers and some are aviation weather forecasters. Pilots will call to get a briefing prior to departure and to file the flight plans that show up as strips at the tower and center.

Unlike IFR, a VFR (Visual Flight Rules) aircraft is not under direct control unless he enters controlled airspace – as in close to a towered airport. The vast majority of the sky below 18,000 feet is "uncontrolled", so a VFR pilot can just take off as long as he avoids controlled airspace.

The reason they may choose to file a flight plan is so that if they have a situation that causes them to land prematurely and cannot contact anyone, Flight Service will institute the Search and Rescue procedures. If someone crashes and survives the initial encounter with mother earth, Flight Service will begin the process of sending out a rescue team as soon as the flight becomes overdue.

The inflight function of Flight Service takes place over the radios. At one time there were over 400 flight service stations – almost all airports of any size boasted one. Advances in technology allowed the FAA to start consolidating them in the late 1980's. A pilot can call Flight Service to activate/amend/ cancel his VFR flight plan, he can get weather updates enroute or he can make other requests that the Center or Towers do not provide.

Flight Service performs a variety of other functions as well – they coordinate information for pilots crossing international borders with Homeland Security and they publish Notices to Airmen (NOTAMs) for airport, flight schools and many other entities. NOTAMs are snippets of information that tell pilots something is not normal. For instance, a NOTAM may say that there is a runway closed at their destination airport, or one of the frequencies along their route is out of service.

Stress is Relative!

Flight Service distributes Pilot Reports (information from airborne aircraft as to what the weather is like at their altitude), and they relay IFR clearances in areas where Center does not have adequate radio coverage.

The Inflight position at Flight Service also helps pilots aloft who are in emergency status – especially lost ones. Some aircraft routinely fly below radar coverage so the ARTCC's and Approach Controls don't "see" them, and if they are students they may get confused as to their location. From the air every lake, mountain and tree tends to look alike in new places. Pilots call the Inflight Radio position at Flight Service – whose people are trained in techniques for helping the pilots become oriented.

VFR pilots are comfortable and familiar with Flight Service, and the history of this branch has always been more friendly and personable than the other two. They will call Flight Service either over the phone or by radio for all kinds of information.

* * * * *

So once again, off I went to the Flight Service school in Oklahoma City. I had been recruited to go to Gallup, NM as my first duty station, but someone who wanted to go there asked if they could switch with me and I ended up in El Paso, TX. (I was more than happy to switch a very small town for one that had a university and a thriving arts community)

This time when I went to the Academy it would have required my daughters to change schools four times in one school year, so my generous and loving parents offered to have the girls live with them in Indiana. My youngest sister, Loretta, was still living at home as well so she participated in molding them into the wonderful women they are.

* * * * *

Stress is Relative!

My third trip to the Academy began in November and ended the next March. Another woman from Albuquerque Tower was assigned to the same class, so we decided to become roommates. We left Albuquerque the day after a massive ice storm had ripped through the high desert – it took three days to do what should have been a nine hour drive.

When we left Albuquerque on Monday, the skies were blue and the sun bright, but the ice was three inches thick along I-40. There were vehicles off the side of the road everywhere – mostly trucks that had not had the sense to park someplace until the storm passed.

There were 14 moving trucks from national chains jackknifed – 13 of them from the same company. One of the trucks had flipped and rolled tearing open the container – some poor person's entire household goods and furniture were scattered over a quarter mile radius.

The traffic was dense and moving very slowly. After 13 hours of driving we stopped and spent the night in Tucumcari. The next day we only made it across the Texas Panhandle and spent the night in Elk City, Oklahoma. Finally, we got to OKC around noon of the third day.

Each evening we called the tower from our hotels (this was before cell phones) to tell them our predicament and they kept the Academy informed of our progress. We were somewhat worried that they would make us go back and begin with a later class if we arrived late, but they understood.

It turned out that there was another two people on their way to the Academy from California behind us on I-40 who did not make it. They went back home and were assigned a later class.

The FAA Academy always announces at the beginning of every new class that they will have class every single week day – the Academy never closes! This is not true. I have been there twice when severe winter storms closed the place down for a couple days.

* * * * *

Stress is Relative!

After having successfully completed the ARTCC training, and the Radar courses, I was quite familiar with the Air Traffic Control Academy at this point. I had also developed enough confidence in myself that no one was going to try and harass me in any way or slip one over on me.

The classwork was easy. The simulations for orienting lost aircraft and performing flight data/search and rescue functions were a cinch. There was one old geezer, an evaluator who liked to frequent strip joints who tried to throw me for a loop during one of the graded simulations.

In the middle of the simulation I was waiting for my next call to drop in when he said to me, "You know, I heard that Johnny Wad passed away."

Johnny Wad was the stage name of a famous XXX rated porn star.

I didn't say anything, so he went on. "I saw him interviewed on TV once, he said that the only thing he ever really wanted to do in life was drive a truck."

Without batting an eyelash I said "I thought he did." Then I answered an incoming call and finished the simulation.

The evaluator started laughing/choking as quietly as he could. He didn't dare give me less than 100% on that test.

After it was over I was out in the hallway when a classmate, a friend who'd been sitting at the station next to me during that evaluation, pushed me up against the wall and said "Don't you EVER do that to me again!"

"What?" I said.

He continued, "I'm trying to figure out what the heck comes next and you guys are joking about porn stars!"

* * * *

I haven't said as much about the members of this Academy class as I did about the Center class. They all had come through the system in a

Stress is Relative!

similar way. I mentioned before how others in my original class had to drop out for one reason or another and some were allowed to segue into different branches of ATC. Flight Service attracted a lot of them.

Overall, as a group, the Flight Service people I have worked with over the years are far more interesting and easy to work with than the other two options. I have always found friends wherever I went, but when circumstances pushed me into changing my career to Flight Service, I came home.

Since most of them were already vetted we lost very few people during the Flight Service training in Oklahoma City. Over the years I ran into many of these classmates at other aviation events. Since there were a lot more Flight Service facilities than Centers, there was more movement between them.

One thing common to all Air Traffic jobs is that after you become proficient in one place, and you can choose to bid on another one that boasts a higher pay grade. Centers are mostly stable, but tower and flight service personnel tend to move around a lot until they find someplace where the traffic is to their liking and the paycheck is acceptable.

CHAPTER 23

El Paso Flight Service

After the Academy I had to spend a month at Albuquerque Flight Service (ABQ) before I transitioned to El Paso (ELP). ABQ was a much larger facility – a level 3 – than El Paso, which was a level 2. There were still a lot of small Level 1 facilities open at the time, so I felt fortunate. Although I love the countryside and mountains, I really preferred living close to someplace with a university.

El Paso boasted a total of ten journeymen, three supervisors, a secretary and a manager. I went through my OJT quickly and was certified within two months of coming on duty. I really wanted to go back to live in Albuquerque, but needed to build up seniority before I would win a bid up to the higher traffic level facility.

This was a part-time Level 2 Flight Service: open at 5am and close at 10pm. The radios covered the southern third of New Mexico and the West Texas area as far east as Guadalupe. At night the radio and phone responsibilities transferred up to Albuquerque.

The building also housed a local branch of the National Weather Service. They took weather observations and built forecasts for the airport.

Stress is Relative!

El Paso Flight Service Station circa 1989

* * * * *

My daughters were in middle school when we moved there. They both had lovely singing voices and joined the school choir. Melissa's coloratura voice was impressive – she was asked to sing with the local college for a special spring event.

We bought a house in a nice neighborhood not too far from the airport. Being right on the border we traveled across to Juarez Mexico where they had a big farmer's market a few times. Talk about rampant prejudice! They did not like to bargain with women at all!

When I wanted to seriously look at buying special items I asked one of the guys I work with who speaks Spanish to come with me because there were times I would attempt to purchase things and had men turn away.

In El Paso there were neighborhoods close to the border where someone of obviously European descent were snubbed or ignored. I remember visiting a Mexican restaurant there with a friend. We went in for lunch and sat at a booth. When she ordered lunch my friend asked which of the sauces was the least salty. She explained that her doctors wanted her on a low-salt diet.

When the food showed up it was LOADED with salt. She had me taste it and you could swear someone had just opened up the box and poured it on her food. We told the waitress who had no sympathy and insisted we pay for it as it was since we'd taken a couple bites. We went to the manager, who said we had to pay for the drinks (ice tea). All the time we had the sense that we were being deliberately messed with.

Many people fleeing bad economic conditions south of El Paso would sneak across the border to beg in the city. At every streetlight near the border there were men or women with their hands out, or someone with a spray bottle would run up while you were holding at a stoplight and spray your windshield, then wipe it with a dirty rag and hold their hand out like they expected you to pay them for the service.

Even so, I was lucky – it was not for another decade that bullets from Juarez would make their way into the sides and doors of buildings across the river in El Paso.

* * * * *

I continued doing photography – made a nice side income and provided a new source of satisfaction for my artistic soul. I shot pictures for political campaigns and realtors and I even got a contract to shoot pictures for the Amigo Airshow. The Navy Blue Angels performed aerial gymnastics before a crowd of thousands. Dozens of military and civilian aircraft were parked on the ramp alongside tents full of booths. NASA had a great booth where they allowed some folks to don spacesuits while an announcer explained all the fittings.

Stress is Relative!

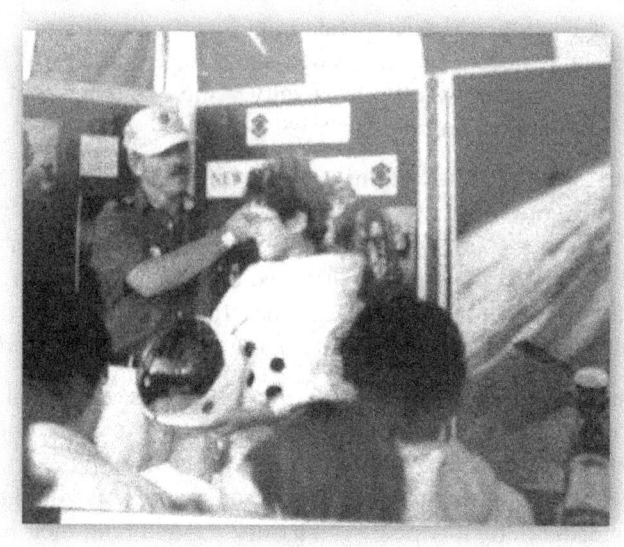

My daughter Carolyn, just thirteen, was chosen to be suited up –
she was smiling from ear to ear!

* * * * *

The pilots for the space shuttle would practice landings at the White Sands Space Harbor just north of El Paso. They would fly in from Ellington Air Force Base in Houston during the week, then an instructor would take them in a specially modified Gulfstream 2 (G2). The G2 aircraft was an executive jet that was modified so that there was standard instrumentation in the cockpit on the right side, but the left side contained the same instrumentation they would be using in the space shuttle.

Stress is Relative!

NASA maintained some of their aircraft at El Paso. One of them was the Guppy – a huge aircraft with a bulbous nose which was used to transport the space shuttle arm. It looked like a whale. You could open up the front section and put the fuselage of a C130 cargo plane inside. The girls and I were allowed to tour it – what fun!

While I was stationed in El Paso, the NASA manager offered to let us ride along during a Shuttle training flight. I jumped at the opportunity!

There is a large piece of airspace north of El Paso over White Sands Missile Range that is restricted to military activities. The White Sands Spaceport is located under that airspace. It was built especially for emergency Shuttle landings, and was otherwise used primarily for practice flights.

Shuttle pilots and their trainers left in the modified G2 aircraft from El Paso and flew north to the restricted airspace. The main fuselage behind the cockpit had standard seating for passengers, but initially I stood in the center section behind the pilots to watch the action. Holding onto the bars set on either side I watched as the instructor pilot climbed to 42,000 feet. Once there he feathered back the engines – essentially turning it into a big glider with limited maneuverability. At this point the Shuttle pilot took over.

As the aircraft began to "fall" he used the control surfaces to turn it towards the airport. The descent angle was so steep that I realized I was looking almost straight down at the airport. I held onto the bars and as we plunged downwards we even became a tad weightless!

The pilot lined up for approach, coming in right over the top of the five mile long gypsum runway. Before the wheels could touch down, at the place where if he was actually in the shuttle his wheels would be touching down, his instructor kicked the engines back up and we began our climb back up to the flight levels.

The pilots would do this about ten to twelve times per training session. The G forces produced were tiring – I could only take three times before I had to go sit down in the back. But they have to be able to land the aircraft after a long space flight, so they train beyond the level of "tired".

It was a fascinating experience. Little was I to know that at a date twenty years in the future I would be even more involved with this activity.

*****

At El Paso Flight Service we had a teletype machine that would print out the weather advisory information from the National Weather Service. On the wall hung huge maps of the southern half of New Mexico and the western portions of Texas. The maps were covered in Plexiglas.

Stress is Relative!

We took grease pencils and drew lines to represent the areas of adverse weather – AIRMETs or SIGMETs for turbulence were drawn in yellow. Red was for IFR low cloud conditions, brown for Mountain Obscuration, white for icing. Each was labeled with the relevant data on altitudes and intensities.

We had another chart for the thunderstorm information and Area Weather Watches for severe weather. Three times a day we would use a smelly white liquid to clean off the old data and post the most recent data sent to us.

The NWS also sent charts via a DIFAX machine - surface analysis, weather depiction, and prognosis (forecast). These were about 18 inches tall by 24 inches wide, and we would post them on the wall so everyone could see them. The DIFAX used the same chemical components and types of paper as a mimeograph – the smell was sharp and tangy.

We could get the current conditions on the Model 1 Full Capacity computer. Glowing green letters on a black screen updated the METARs and forecasts and whatever NOTAMs we requested. Most of our notes and records were kept on paper in those days.

The facility was located next to the general aviation FBO's (fixed base operators). FBOs are independently owned businesses where pilots park, get fuel and maintenance. Pilots could easily walk over to our building to do their flight planning rather than call on the phone.

El Paso Airport had really deep basins dug between the runways. There isn't a lot of rain in the desert, but when the "monsoons" hit in July through September the sheer amount of water can easily cause flooding. Most places don't have underground drainage systems but the roads are tilted so water runs towards these big open basins. Since it is mostly sand, the water percolates down into the aquifer fairly quickly.

El Paso seldom sees snow – maybe once every five or six years – and it doesn't last long. The summers get very hot – one year we had daily temperatures of 105 degrees three weeks straight.

The only word that you need to describe the springtime is WIND.

Stress is Relative!

When the wind rips unblocked across the desert, the sand and dust spew upwards a thousand feet or more. Visibility on the surface can become nil.

One spring the winds blew up to 68 knots across the airport for over an hour. You could not see six feet outside the back door. When they finally subsided one of my co-workers looked outside and said, "Wasn't there a DC3 parked over there?"

Sure enough, the old air carrier was missing. The wind had picked it up and pushed it backwards. It was found at the bottom of the large water catchment basin between the parking ramp and Runway 04/22.

Stress is Relative!

CHAPTER 24

Striding Towards Diversity

El Paso was the first facility I worked in where the government placed new people who had not been through the Academy and standard training in an effort to promote equality in the workforce. Having seen the paucity of diversity in the job first hand, I know the reasons for the "special programs", but the outcomes were debatable in terms of success.

The Hispanic population of El Paso was high, so the FAA opened up a "recruiting blitz" there and in other southern cities. They advertised that seminars would be held in those locations to go over the Air Traffic Control entrance exam, hoping this would attract women and minorities. I was one of the volunteer instructors.

The workshop could not be closed to any particular group, and predictably there were not as many minorities as we were hoping for, but there were some. Shortly after the workshop, the entrance exam was given in El Paso – most anyone who took the workshop did well. They still had to go through the rest of the application process and the Academy in order to advance.

Another group of people came into the job through the "Pre-Developmental" program. Many women and minorities were given tours of all the ATC facilities and some base aviation training. But then they

Stress is Relative!

were sent directly to an ATC facility to see how they would do rather than going through the Academy.

Some of them did well, some didn't, just like in any situation. We had a few Pre-D's at El Paso FSS, and they learned the job well. I met others over time who did not do well, and relied on others to pick up after them. This was really problematic because many times a person who was simply not "getting it" would complain that they were being unfairly treated because of their race or sex, when they simply could not handle the job.

Of course, even with the standard training progression, not everyone who entered the profession in the usual way succeeded in attaining their goals. With the truncated program it seemed that the balance between safety and fairness was difficult to maintain as the federal government made a concerted effort to diversify.

* * * * *

There was another factor as well. Most of the women I have met in my profession who made it all the way through to full performance level in their fields are very strong, practical, intelligent and independently minded people. However, as in any job, there were some who frankly made me cringe because their actions reflected badly on all the other women who were fighting to gain respect in a male dominated society.

One example is a woman I'll call Janine. She was petite and pretty, and married – a status that did not interfere with her love life. Her shift started very early in the day – usually 5am. As more people came on duty later in the morning after the rush we would sometimes do a "chow run". Unlike the Center, the FSS was smaller so there was no cafeteria – but we were in the heart of town and there were a lot of fast food restaurants nearby.

Janine would come to work in a tight leather mini-skirt, low cut blouse and four inch heels. During the slack time in the morning she would be chatting up the guys and in a little girl voice say "I'm so hunnnnngry."

Inevitably one of the guys would say, "Hey, no problem…I'll do a chow run."

Stress is Relative!

Then she'd say "but I didn't bring any money."

The guy would offer to pay for something for her then ask if anyone else wanted something and get permission from the supervisor to take a break long enough to run out and get food. This went on several times a week.

During the course of the day she would whine about being cold as she flipped her long hair behind her, and once, when a supervisor was telling her he'd heard complaints about her comportment from other specialists she said "The other women are just jealous because I'm the prettiest".

Really?

That kind of behavior augments the outdated belief that women are unsuitable in just about any workforce much less Air Traffic Control. It has often been said that a woman must be better than a man in the same job in order to be considered equal. This was also true of a woman's personal conduct. We were constantly under scrutiny and the flaws of one woman could be touted as gender shortcomings.

* * * * *

As I mentioned, El Paso was a small facility. It shared the building with the National Weather Service. The NWS staff was all male.

The building had a large restroom for the men – it contained showers as well as toilet facilities; but the women's restroom had been added as an afterthought. It was a converted storage closet. Since there was just one stall it had a lock on the door.

One of the NWS guys thought it would be great fun to harass me when I went to the ladies room. He waited for me to go in, then went up to the hollow core metal door and slapped it hard with his open palm. It made a very loud BOOM in that small space.

It had the desired effect, I jumped and yelped.

He ran back to his area and bragged to the guys about "scaring the shit" out of me.

Stress is Relative!

I exited the room and a friend of mine was at the preflight desk. I said "Who did that?" My friend, Bob, pointed at the NWS office.

As I entered the Weather guys were all gathered around listening to the culprit and laughing. As I said before I am not one who wants to get other people in trouble, but I don't like being the target of practical jokes like that either, so I smiled and quietly said "Ok, you had your little joke. I am warning you, don't do it again."

Of course, a few days later he did it again.

Bob was on duty again and had seen him do it. Inwardly seething, I immediately went up to the supervisor, on duty, Salvadore, and asked him to pull the forms to file an official EEO complaint. Sal got them out and I started to fill them out. I had justification and I had witnesses.

In the meantime the other guys at the NWS were urgently telling the perpetrator that he'd better get over to our office and apologize big time. It finally sank in when his boss told him that his actions were a firing offense.

The paperwork was done and about to be signed when the jerk came into the office and apologized profusely to me in front of a lot of people. Like I said, I don't really want to hurt people. I showed him the paperwork and told him that I would not file it right now…but if he ever did that or anything else mean spirited to me or anyone I worked with again – I would take the form out of my locker and send it in.

He must have believed me because he behaved after that.

* * * * *

I've often wondered why some guys feel compelled to do stupid, hurtful things like that. To me that kind of stunt is done by small minded people with an inferiority complex trying pathetically to get attention.

Stress is Relative!

The Space Shuttle traveling from where it landed after a mission on the west coast to the Kennedy Space Center atop a B747. It routinely stopped for fuel at Biggs Army Airfield – which was located adjacent to El Paso International Airport.

Stress is Relative!

Rose working the Preflight Briefing position
at El Paso Flight Service (ELP FSS)

Stress is Relative!

CHAPTER 25

Working in ELP FSS

Most of the people I worked with in El Paso were great. They were competent in the job and always jumped in when someone needed a hand. Usually about six journeymen worked during the day shift and three or four in the evenings.

As I mentioned, one of the functions of Flight Service is to help VFR pilots become oriented when they get lost. The vast majority of pilots who fly VFR are general aviation as opposed to commercial, executive or military. Many of them are students.

We had three flight schools in our area – one at Biggs Army Airfield nearby, one at El Paso Airport and a large international school at Las Cruces about 40 miles west of El Paso. The North American Institute of Aviation (NAIA) catered primarily to European students.

In those days the instructors routinely taught the students to call Flight Service and pretend they were lost as part of their training – so we did practice DF steers at least twice a week.

A DF, or Direction Finder, was a line of sight piece of equipment that tuned in on the pilot's radio signal and displayed a direction from its location to the aircraft. It was one of the methods we used when the aircraft was flying too low to be picked up by the ARTCC or Approach radars.

Stress is Relative!

We had one DF site at El Paso, another to the east at Guadalupe, TX and one sited to the north at Truth or Consequences, NM. If the pilot's frequency could be picked up by at least two of them we had a good cross fix.

We would determine his location on the map and tell him where he was and then ask what he wanted – which was usually a heading to his destination airport.

* * * * *

Working El Paso Radio one day a student from the North American Institute of Aviation Flight School called who really was quite lost. While tuning the DF I asked him where he thought he was – he said "Deming?" Deming is a town about 60 miles west of El Paso.

When the signals came back and I plotted his location he was 35 miles southeast of El Paso – in Mexico.

Immediately my team went to work. While I spoke to the kid, calming him down and having him turn north to get him back into the United States, Salvadore called U.S. Customs so they would not think he was a drug dealer sneaking across the border, Bob called El Paso Approach control, and Barb called the flight school.

I had him squawk emergency (transponder code 7700) so that El Paso approach control would see him as soon as he came into range. He was low on fuel at that time so we had him get across the border and over to a small airport east of El Paso International right away. He landed safely, but was shaken enough that the flight school sent an instructor to help him fly home.

* * * * *

Another memorable DF event happened when a Bonanza (small single engine aircraft) pilot flying from Midland, Texas to El Paso called. I identified his position and asked his intentions. He said "Are there any airports around here? I need to land." I found him a small one at Fabens, TX just thirty miles to the north.

"I see it." He said. "Thanks, my passenger just vomited all over my console and I can't read the instruments."

* * * * *

Being a small facility, El Paso flight service was the first place where I witnessed antagonism between the facility manager and the FSS union representative first hand. The manager had grown up in the El Paso area and like most in ATC had worked in several other locations before finally ending his career as Chief of the facility in his home town. He projected a "Big Man on Campus" attitude.

The facility union rep was also from the local area – and hated the manager. This did not make for a serene working environment.

This manager enjoyed lording it over the workforce. He defined the dress code to suit himself. One day a lady wore open toed shoes to work – he sent her home to change them because they were too suggestive.

Managers of smaller facilities like El Paso are supposed to maintain their operational currency so they can work a position like everyone else in cases where the staffing is short. One time there were several people legitimately on sick leave when an employee called to say they'd fallen and broken their arm so they would not be coming to work that afternoon.

This would have left the operations floor short, so the manager called the specialist with the broken arm and told him sick leave was NOT allowed and to get his butt into work. He was not about to lower himself to work operations.

The manager frequently came into work with a sack of breakfast food in the morning. He'd go directly into the break room to sit and eat – while the supervisors came to him to update him on what was happening in the facility.

Stress is Relative!

After breakfast he'd disappear into his office for a couple hours, then he'd tell the secretary he was going to have lunch with "the chief of Juarez Flight Service", which was 10 miles south of the border in Mexico.

In other words, he and his buddy were going to play golf for a few hours. He may or may not actually show up at the facility later in the day for an hour or two.

The union rep tried to inform the FAA that the El Paso manager was falsifying his timecard. Unfortunately, their investigator showed up on a day when the union rep was not working. Most of us on duty were fairly new to the facility so we didn't have the records he collected.

The union rep loved nothing more than to goad the manager every chance he could get.

One morning the manager came in with his breakfast and sat in his usual chair in front of the TV – right in a puddle of honey. As soon as he felt it he jumped up yelling for and at the union rep – assuming he was the guilty party.

The union rep swaggered into the room admitting nothing, but smiling. The manager was so angry he started towards the union rep with his fists at the ready. Luckily for him one of the supervisors stepped between them and broke it up before any fisticuffs began.

One of the few ways to get fired in the FAA was to physically strike a fellow employee.

* * * * *

Every so often a bid would come out for Albuquerque Flight Service. I had never really wanted to be anywhere else, I love Albuquerque. I love the way the sunsets color Sandia Mountain a screaming hot pink.

Stress is Relative!

My Mother had given up on the idea that I would ever move back to Indiana by this time. I missed her and Dad and would either drive or fly back for visits at least twice a year. It seemed like every time I went back I became more uncomfortable with the humidity and my allergies to everything in bloom frequently made the trip miserable.

Others with more seniority would get the bid for the first couple years. In my third year I finally won the bid. I packed up the girls, put the house on the market and moved north.

Stress is Relative!

Albuquerque Automated Flight Service Station

1992

Stress is Relative!

CHAPTER 26

Albuquerque Flight Service

I went on duty at Albuquerque Automated Flight Service (ABQ AFSS) in November of 1991. One year earlier the FAA had moved the people and equipment into a brand new building on the southwest side of the airfield near the General Aviation Area. The old adobe one was falling apart and was demolished a year after Flight Service moved.

ABQ was a Hub facility. It had backups to the frequencies for all the other, smaller flight service facilities in New Mexico and southwest Texas. When the small ones closed at night the ABQ personnel took over responsibility for those airports.

Since communications technology was improving daily, the FAA had determined that hundreds of smaller flight services could be closed with no loss of service. All the phone lines and radios were relayed by microwave links to the larger facilities.

The essence of what Flight Service had been to the general aviation community was changing. When there was an FSS at airports of any size a pilot could walk in the building and talk to the people on duty and look at the weather maps themselves. The FSS was a place where pilots would sometimes gather and talk about their passions for flying and aircraft, kinda like an old country store.

Stress is Relative!

This meant that the FSS personnel were deeply involved in the local aviation community – if "one of theirs" had an inflight emergency or went missing they went to lengths over and beyond the written requirements to help them. Flight Service was the branch of the FAA that pilots felt comfortable with and since the FSS phone lines are the only ones in ATC that are published, pilots call it whenever they need questions answered.

I have heard stories of pilots landing at a smaller airport located some distance from town where there were no facilities other than an FSS and a fuel truck. At several locations, the airfield was a couple miles from the nearest restaurant, so the Flight Service specialist might offer the pilot the use of her car – she tossed him the keys and he tossed her the keys to his airplane.

* * * * *

Stress is Relative!

Flight Service was, and is, the FAA's primary and most immediate line of communication with the General Aviation community. At one point in time there were FSS facilities at over 400 airports – always located on the airport grounds.

Just about anyone who works in this field has spoken to one or more pilots who experienced fatal crashes, and we have all worked inflight emergencies. It is part of our monthly training to go over the various scenarios which could cause a pilot to become disoriented and lost, or what to do if one called in a panic because he's got smoke in the cockpit or an engine conked out.

That's where keeping an even tone while talking to them pays out – being calm helps the pilot to focus and hopefully find a way to land safely.

One day I gave a briefing to a pilot who was VFR only. This meant that he could not fly in clouds at all. He really wanted to get to New Braunfels, Texas. I told him VFR flight was not recommended and gave him the weather data proving that the clouds were down to around a hundred feet off the ground – or less – across the last third of his route of flight.

I remember he said, "No problems, I can fly just above the treetops."

I heard he crashed about 50 miles west of his destination.

We always wonder in that situation, is there any way we could have convinced the pilot not to fly that day? Could we have done or said anything that would have changed his mind? As long as we've given the pilots all the information at our disposal we are not legally or morally liable, but darn it, that was a person who was alive and talking to me just a few hours ago.

Although icing is the leading cause of weather related aircraft accidents, thunderstorms are a close second. Many small aircraft pilots feel they can fly under a thunderstorm out west because the bases of the clouds are high in mountainous areas. But that is deceptive as the storm

Stress is Relative!

activity generates a lot of unpredictable, strong downdrafts which can swat an aircraft like a fly.

When we felt a pilot was really being nonchalant about heading into an intense weather situation many FSS specialists would come up with verbiage that was not exactly approved to describe how bad it was. Occasionally you'd hear things like:

> "Sir, could you please name me as primary beneficiary on your insurance before you go?"
>
> "Those are not clouds you see along the route, they are Cumulous Granite – turn around and fly back into the valley!"
>
> "...and who is your next of kin?"
>
> "I suggest you call back in ten minutes and talk to someone else because I don't want to be the last person to speak to you before you die."
>
> The best one I heard of was from a guy at Baton Rouge Flight Service in Louisiana who was trying to tell a student pilot how strong the storm system was.
>
> "You nail your G__...D____....A___ to the ground and don't even think about taking off!"

Stress is Relative!

* * * * *

In addition to the usual charts and other training involved in changing facilities, I got to learn Albuquerque's newest computer system. They still had the old M1FC computer when I first got there, but they did not have to draw weather information on a big wall board – they had computer with GRAPHICAL IMAGES!

The WSI downloaded radar and satellite imagery directly through the NWS as well as pictorially displaying the boundaries of the weather advisories, the winds aloft patterns, and all the other information that we had to visualize from written text in the past! What a concept!

In today's world anyone can pull up a weather website and have pictures and graphics far superior to what we started with, but in those days it was a tiny, welcome glimpse into the future. No more drawing lines on walls or ripping off big paper charts from the smelly machine, then posting the charts on the wall so everyone could jump up and go look at them.

* * * * *

By the turn of the century all the smaller Flight Service Stations in the lower 48 states had closed and all their frequencies, phone numbers and people combined into the larger hubs. I had gone back to college and finished my degree so I could bid on supervisory and staff jobs, but the FAA/union rules still preferred to promote based on seniority rather than performance. Every year I was given exceptional ratings in my annual review.

This was the first facility I worked in that was at least 20% female. Here I didn't have very many problems with harassment. Only once, shortly after I got there, did a guy try something inappropriate.

I was in the break room getting lunch when an old guy grabbed my ass. Without thinking I whipped around, pushed him up against the

Stress is Relative!

refrigerator and said intently, "If you ever do that again I will have your job."

Then I finished making my sandwich. He never bothered me after that and since no one had been there to witness either action nothing was ever said about it.

Guess I had graduated from the FAA's assertiveness training pretty well by that time.

* * * * *

Training and certification at Albuquerque Flight Service was a breeze. My area of responsibility encompassed the whole state of New Mexico – with which I was very familiar. After a year or so one of the coveted "Flight Watch" positions came open. Flight Watch personnel had to take extra classes and be certified by the National Weather Service as Aviation Weather Forecasters. The job did not include any extra pay, but it was a standard stepping stone to staff and supervisory levels.

It also meant that your work schedule was adjusted so that at least two Flight Watch specialists were constantly on duty from 6am to 10pm daily. Normally you rotate from Inflight to Flight Data to Pilot Briefing during your work week, now I just added some hours working Flight Watch.

We got some kidding from the others at the facility – they called us the "Flight Watch Gods", but for the most part it was just another job function.

* * * * *

Things didn't change much for a decade after I transferred to Albuquerque. Finally I was in the place I wanted to be both physically and professionally.

During this time my daughters graduated high school and I took up gardening and volunteering for various non-profit groups.

Stress is Relative!

I met my future husband, who also worked at Albuquerque Flight Service. I went back to college and finished my degree in non-profit administration – it actually came in useful later on

I was at a point in my life where the battles were all done and I could just enjoy being. Or so I thought.

* * * * *

Many Flight Service folk decided to change facilities rather than retire when the smaller places closed, so for a while Flight Service was top heavy with people. There were no new people coming in– and since Flight Service is the only branch of ATC that does not have mandatory retirement at age 55 there were few who left during this period. This meant that the seniority list stayed static.

In the past you could work your way up in seniority as people on top retired and new people hired in. Being on the bottom of the list meant the worst choice of shifts and days off (we were a 24 hour facility), and you had the last pick of available vacation dates.

Most people wanted to have Friday/Saturday as their days off because that meant they could earn an extra 25% for working on Sundays and still be free for one weekend day. Naturally the oldest, most senior people got those days – EVERY YEAR. The new ones, who usually were the ones with kids at home, ended up with mid-week days off. A lot of them also had to take the evening and midnight shifts in most facilities.

Each FSS could set up their own schedules to an extent through the unions. Because working from 6pm to 6am earned an extra 10% and Sundays an extra 25%, these shifts were prized. In facilities where the desire for premium shifts ran high the FAA would require specialists to work rotating shifts with rotating days off – a truly killer schedule.

In other places, like ABQ where the specialists preferred stable lifestyles the union could set up schedules with fixed days off – bid

Stress is Relative!

once a year – with either all day shifts, all evenings, all mids and/or a few "rattlers" where someone did two evenings, two days and a mid each week.

I preferred having mid-week days off. This was good since I was at that facility for almost ten years before I was any higher than 3rd from the bottom of the seniority list. Tuesday and Wednesday off meant I came back in on evening shifts Thursday and Friday, then worked days on Saturday and Sunday, then either a day or a midshift on Monday. I could get off work by 2pm on Monday afternoon and not go back to work until Thursday at 4pm – almost three days off each week!

Midweek days off are great – no lines at the grocery stores, easy to set up medical and other appointments, and you could choose to work another part time job if you liked. In my case I was still doing photography and I also volunteered for several organizations. .

The shift I liked best were midnights – 10pm to 6am. Sleeping during the day was not usually a problem, and by the time I got to Albuquerque my kids were in high school. I was one of four specialists who worked straight mids for a number of years until the Roswell FSS closed and someone with higher seniority than I turned up who wanted the midshift.

* * * * *

Over the 1990's the FAA closed down all the smaller facilities and combined them into larger Hubs so that what was left was approximately one per state, with the exception of Alaska. Level one facilities where only a few people worked closed first. The employees were given a choice, they could stay in their communities and retire or they could be transferred to the Hub. Those who still needed to work moved at the government's expense.

* * * * *

Stress is Relative!

The only problem I had with midnight shifts were people wanting to knock on your door during the day for some reason – usually sales types or church representatives. I put a sign on my door that asked people not to ring the doorbell between certain times of the day as the occupant was asleep.

One day there was a knock at the door and my dog went ballistic, barking to raise the roof. I stumbled to the front door without my glasses and there were two guys in suits with bibles under their arms. They immediately went into their pitch and I waved at the sign and said "Can't you read?"

One of them said "We didn't ring the bell, we knocked."

That was so inane I could come up with absolutely no response except to close the door.

Stress is Relative!

The Albuquerque AFSS logo

CHAPTER 27

I Have a Social Life!

I now had a house in the place I wanted to call home, and I was comfortable in my job. The girls were teenagers and both of them were fast becoming self-sufficient. It was a good time to become involved with various elements of the Albuquerque community. I reached out into the local community to do some volunteer work. Having erratic shifts still interfered with performing on stage, but I did get involved with the local community theater in a backstage capacity.

One year I was a stage hand for a production of "Phantom" being performed at Popejoy Hall – a large theater on the University of New Mexico campus. Twenty minutes into the second half the building's fire alarm sounded.

I heard the alarm faintly behind the loud orchestra music and ran over to the stage manager's podium to ask if she heard something.

Connie saw me coming. She had a wild kind of look in her eyes. Behind her the main curtain was rapidly descending as she shoved a microphone in my hand.

"It's live", she said. "Tell them to leave."

Then Connie ran off to make sure the actors and other stagehands exited the building. I figured she meant that I was to tell the audience what to do, so I took a deep breath.

Stress is Relative!

"Ladies and Gentlemen" I could hear my voice carrying to the crowd of over 3,000 people in the audience. "As you can hear we have a fire alarm going off. At this time we have no indication of an actual fire in the auditorium, but fire regulations dictate that we must empty the building. Please make your way to the nearest exit. Once the situation is resolved we will return and finish the production."

It turned out to be a prank, but later, as we were all standing around waiting for the fire marshal to finish his inspection, I approached Connie and asked why she had me do the announcement.

She shook her head and opened her hands, "When I heard the alarm I was panicky, and I knew if I said it the people would hear that in my voice and they might panic too. Then I saw you and something in my head said "Rose is an air traffic controller, she can handle the stress…give it to her."

Wow, what a commentary on how the public perceives my profession!

* * * * *

The lack of women in the field is and was, I feel, primarily attributed to a lack of exposure to it as a career option when they are young.

Aviation in general is something you don't really consider as a career unless you have a parent or relative doing it. It is a visible and attainable option for those who join the military. That is where most people in the job came from before the strike and since more men went into the military than women, the number of controllers who are male was proportionately high.

Can women do the job?
DUH!

Stress is Relative!

ATC is cerebral, not something based on physical strength or even agility. I know several women who received national awards for their work in ATC. It is also something that is a great career option for many who have some kind of physical handicap that requires a wheelchair as long as they are in the Center or Flight Service options. (Towers require you to climb stairs)

One of our best specialists at Albuquerque Flight Service was paraplegic. Marlin sat in a wheelchair but he was great at his job. I admired his ability to maintain a strict diet – passing up Christmas cookies for instance. I remember he told me that it was important to regulate his weight - since he moves around using his arms he couldn't let himself get fat.

I began speaking at career days for the middle schools and high schools around the city. I had a video tape showing what Air Traffic Controllers do – it followed a flight from departure to destination. Since I was actually doing the job I could answer a lot of questions and was happy to see interest in the eyes of all the students.

There was only one time that I was caught unprepared by a question. A young woman of about 13 told me that she had epilepsy and was asking if she'd be allowed to be a controller.

That stopped me for a moment, should I just say "I don't know" or tell her the truth. This girl looked like she was very aware of what she should expect, and wanted me to tell her what she needed to know.

I told her that I was no expert, but that controllers and pilots both must pass a Class A airmen's physical examination. I mentioned there were jobs in staff positions which did not require medical certification she could pursue.

I still felt rotten.

* * * * *

Stress is Relative!

Shortly after I moved back to Albuquerque I met a lady whose friendship directed me into a whole new mindset about life.

Elaine could have been a sister – Like me she grew up catholic back in the Midwest and circumstances carried her to New Mexico. Though she was a couple years older than I, her son, Keith, was only three years old when I met her, where mine were teenagers.

Elaine and her husband, Mike, were heavily involved in the New Mexico Solar Energy Association (NMSEA). Their house was situated inside the Albuquerque city limits, near the university, and they had a full solar electrical array in their yard.

We met at a friend's birthday party, and we started talking about environmental options. Elaine introduced me NMSEA and I spent a huge chunk of my spare time working with them over the next decade.

I was taken with the idea of solar cooking and became very good at it. I wrote and published a Solar Cookbook which is still in print called "The Solar Chef". It was my first effort at writing anything for publication.

My work in aviation weather gave me insights into ways of determining the best conditions for cooking dinner using only sunlight and a black box.

A National Solar Energy conference took place in town one year. I sat in on a presentation by an NMSEA member who was a solar radiation statistics engineer. Ray had given a presentation on how solar radiation strikes the earth and mentioned that his data showed it to be strongest at about 2pm in each time zone.

After his presentation the moderator, David, made a snide comment that in HIS observations there were always after cloud activity at that time and thunderstorms. He insinuated that Ray's data was incorrect.

I raised my hand, he called on me and I said, "Actually the summer thunderstorm and cloud activity just begin forming around one to two in the afternoon and fully blown thunderstorms are formed an hour or two later."

Stress is Relative!

David pulled himself upright and looking down his nose said "WELL, I am a DOCTOR of ENGINEERING at BERKLEY UNIVERSITY!"

I raised an eyebrow and calmly stated "Geez, I am only an Aviation Weather Forecaster who looks at real live satellite and radar pictures for eight hours every day....PROFESSOR."

* * * * *

I'd started dating again when I moved to Albuquerque. Most of them were guys I stayed friends with after we decided to call it off. When I finally chose my life companion it was a man with whom I worked.

It was funny because we were friends for years before he casually asked if I wanted to go out to dinner with him after work and things slowly evolved from there. I like the fact that when we talk about work things both of us understand exactly what is being said.

After more than twenty years he is still my best friend.

* * * * *

Something else I finally had the time to do was garden. Since childhood I loved to plants vegetables and flowers, but whenever I had to move for my job whatever was planted was left behind.

There is a Master Gardener program in Albuquerque, so I signed up for the classes to learn about everything from soil types and plant diseases to composting. I bought a chipper/shredder and started piling up chopped up leaves and vegetables.

My husband says I am easier to live with when I have a garden. The work is relaxing to me and whenever I do get stressed out I take a

Stress is Relative!

bunch of tree limbs and run them through the shredder. I like to imagine they are whatever is stressing me.

I got a beehive and set it in my backyard. My house was on half an acre south of town in a semi rural area. The neighbor had a huge garden full of green chili. When I harvested the honey, it had a distinct bite!

* * * * *

Overall, I have felt that the people who worked in Flight Service were much more personable and interesting to work with than in the other ATC places I had been. Many of them, like me, had moved laterally from tower or ARTCC. Others who had retired from ATC in the military were able to transition into Flight Service because it was the only ATC option that allows people to begin their career after the age of 31.

Flight Service people require a larger knowledge base and because they talk to pilots rather than just ordering them around, they are generally friendlier than the other two options – there is not nearly as much competitiveness. The ARTCC and tower people never knew exactly what Flight Service did beyond the areas where the three services overlap, so they didn't realized that it took a great deal more training to work in Flight Service than in their own options.

Stress is Relative!

CHAPTER 28

Emergency Services

Flight Service coordinates search and rescue on overdue aircraft, and it is the FAA facility the pilots call when they get lost or have an inflight emergency.

* * * * *

One evening I took a radio call from a pilot who wanted to land at the Artesia airport south of Roswell, New Mexico. He was trying to lower his landing gear, but the cockpit lights were not indicating the gear was locked in place. He called me.

He did not dare to make a landing until he either had confirmation that the wheels were down or until there was emergency equipment and personnel ready to handle a crash landing. Artesia is a very small airport with no tower, and no emergency equipment on the field. The airport manager and staff had long since gone home for the day.

While I stayed on the radio keeping him calm my supervisor rousted out the local volunteer fire department and sheriff's department while another specialist found the airport managers home phone number and let him know what was going on.

Stress is Relative!

The aircraft, a two engine Beechcraft, circled the airport burning off fuel until the fire trucks and police arrived. He spoke to us through the radios and we relayed to the emergency personnel what his intentions were. Then we all waited quietly when he began his approach to the runway.

He was lucky, the gear was down and locked, though you couldn't tell that in the dark until he landed.

It was one of those instances we are relieved to remember as a non-event.

* * * * *

When a pilot forgets to cancel his flight plan, Flight Service must initiate Search and Rescue half an hour after his ETA – we give him that long to call us just in case he is a little late.

The first step of SAR is usually very easy – you call the destination airport and have the manager or other people on duty take a walk outside to see if that aircraft is parked on the ramp. If he isn't you call the phone number filed on the flight plan and see if whoever answers knows where he is. About 85% of those who are late are found by this point.

If the aircraft is not there then an extensive communications search begins. Flight Service sends messages to all the air traffic facilities from his departure point to destination to see if any of them had contact with the aircraft, and begin plotting out all the airports the pilot could have landed at within fifty miles either side of his route of flight.

If no one has heard from him within the first two hours we begin calling every public use airport large and small to see if he landed short, and we give the national Rescue Coordination Center (RCC) a heads up call.

The RCC then organizes the physical search. They will call up military and civilian aircraft to comb the route of flight to see if they can find wreckage.

Stress is Relative!

Statistics show that if someone has to crash land and manages to survive the initial impact, their chances of survival increase dramatically if they are found within 24 hours.

When the pilots do not cancel their flight plans on time, it could just be that they forgot to – so Flight Service will pull any audio they have to try and figure out what happened before we have to go to the extreme of launching search parties.

I remember once where an aircraft went overdue just after midnight. It was inbound to a small airport - Clovis, New Mexico. We dispatched the sheriff to check the ramps there, but no joy. So we started waking up sheriff's and managers all along the route as usual.

My friend, Harry said, "You know, he's got a really different last name…maybe his relatives know where he is."

We called information and discovered someone with the same last name in the nearby town of Portales. We woke that person up at 3am, and he confirmed that yes, he knew our missing pilot – it was his son who was at that moment asleep in the next room. The son had diverted from landing at his home strip of Clovis to Portales – then put the aircraft into a hanger, making it impossible for the sheriff to find it on the airfield.

As a side note, all of us in Flight Service are very grateful for the law enforcement officers who we've had to call on to drive to a tiny remote airport in the middle of the night just to check and see if an aircraft is sitting there on the ground.

* * * * *

During the years spent in Flight Service I got to know a lot of pilots, and have had the pleasure of going for rides with them in their small aircraft. Though I never took lessons to become a pilot myself, I did join the local pilot's associations and kept abreast of what kinds of things are important to them. .

Stress is Relative!

Some of the professional pilots would call every day at the same time for their briefings. Since they would fly the same aircraft every day along the exact same route, I memorized a lot of the flight plans and would enter the data automatically as I heard their voice.

One of the local box haulers, Jane, flew a C414 from Albuquerque to Roswell to Carlsbad and back every day. FedEx and UPS would bring huge aircraft full of boxes into Albuquerque International in the middle of the night and their personnel would distribute them to the little local carriers to take around the state.

Jane had the Flight Service pilot briefing number on speed dial on her phone next to her bed. One morning I took a call from her at 4am.

"Albuquerque Flight Service." I answered.

A groggy voice spoke. "Hi…It's Jane."

That is all I needed – in thirty seconds her flight plan was in the computer and I had pulled all the data for her briefing. Halfway through I heard "OOOOOfffph!"

"What's the matter?" I asked.

"Nothing….the cat jumped on my stomach."

Stress is Relative!

CHAPTER 29

Technology Jumps

In 2002 the ABQ Flight Service operations room changed dramatically as the FAA installed a new computer system called OASIS. This one computer system had both graphics and textual products in the windows design mode! It set a new standard that other, later systems were measured against.

Over time the radio and communications systems and the computers used by ATC all became more efficient and more flexible. We started getting requests for preflight briefings via cell phone for the first time. Cell phones were annoying when the pilot decided to use them for briefing while standing outside in a high wind, but they were very helpful when it came to search and rescue.

The Center Radars across the country improved to the point that the old DF equipment used by Flight Service to find lost aircraft was determined to be obsolete and was removed everywhere except Alaska.

Slowly the need to keep paper records was reduced as the computers began storing the information automatically. The FAA is required to keep all paperwork and audio recordings for 15 days. If during that time there is an accident, then the information related to the accident will be held onto for up to 2.5 years, but otherwise it is destroyed.

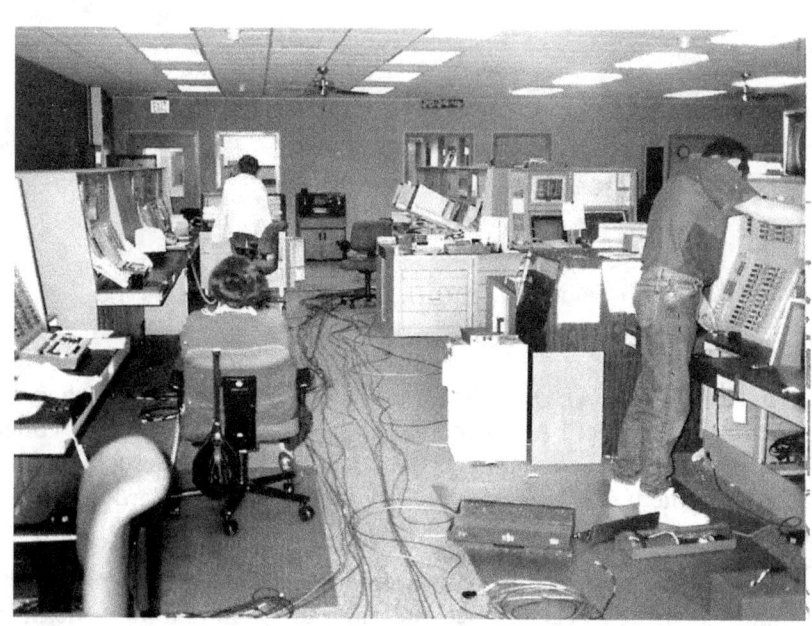

Wires were strung along the floor between consoles as technicians installed the OASIS system while we were working.

* * * * *

Technology made further leaps as we turned the century. One of the primary duties of Flight Service was to file flight plans – for all kinds of aircraft. Air Carriers installed computer links to the FAA so they could file their own flight plans and get weather briefings, so they no longer called us unless their computer went down.

Personal computers were quickly becoming a must have item for any home, and if you could afford to buy an aircraft – even a small one – you could afford a computer. Several websites were devoted to

Stress is Relative!

weather in general and others quickly popped up that were dedicated to aviation weather, including the National Weather service site: www.aviationweather.gov.

Then the FAA contracted a service called DUATS which allowed pilots to file their own flight plans through a website.

Those of us who kept up on these breakthroughs began to speculate that Flight Service had to change. Services that had been inherently part of our job were now able to be performed by anyone.

* * * * *

Specialists working in ABQ AFSS Operations

Stress is Relative!

Inflight (Radio) console with 60 frequencies on the left.

Stress is Relative!

CHAPTER 30

Life at the Albuquerque Flight Service Station

Sometimes a supervisor needs to spend the time in his office catching up on paperwork. When this happens he designates a CIC, or Controller in Charge.

We used to make up a lot of meanings for CIC....Chump in Charge, Chick in Charge, and because we worked in New Mexico it might be a Chicano in Charge. As long as no one was offended we could do that.

And that is where we were in the '90's. I already mentioned we had quite a few women at ABQ AFSS, we also had a high percentage of Hispanics and a few Native Americans. There was only one person of African American descent which was proportionate to the population diversity of the region.

I came from Indiana where there is a much higher percentage of African Americans, but when I left there were very few other races. New Mexico was and is a fascinating blend of cultures, races and religions. They don't call Santa Fe the "city different" for nothing!

Terms and slang you used in your childhood without thinking deeply about them have different meanings in a new location.

One day a technician wanted to work on one of my radio frequencies. I gave him permission and reached up to turn it off. He had tried to do that earlier, but that area was busy enough that I had to tell him no.

Joking, he said, "You're not going to take it back are you?"

I responded, "No, I am not an Indian giver!" And we both laughed.

Some month's later I was called into the Chief's office because a different person entirely who happened to overhear the conversation had filed an EEO complaint against me because of the term "Indian giver".

I had never considered that this was a term someone might think offensive. In my perspective it referred to the government's practice of giving land to the Indians and later taking it back. However, what the Native American's hear is a nuance of the phrase indicating that you can't trust someone to give something to you and let you keep it if they were Indian. Of course I apologized and it was over quickly, but it did make me realize that I needed to think about what I said and not just assume that everyone had the same understandings as I did.

* * * * *

As I mentioned earlier, ABQ AFSS was the first place I worked where there were more women in the controller workforce. Most of them were strong, intelligent, and extremely capable individuals, a true pleasure to work with.

I remember one rare evening when I was the "Chick in Charge" at the supervisor's desk, looking up and realizing that besides myself, LuAnne was working Flight Watch, Georgie was at Inflight, Brooke was at Flight Data, Sherry and Mary were pre-flight briefing. An all-girl team!

The next morning in a deadpan voice, I told the facility chief that the building had been unmanned for several hours the previous day. He exclaimed "WHAT!?"

Stress is Relative!

Every specialist rotated through the various jobs during the day, which involved physically moving to a new location. One day there happened to be three women and one man in the northeast quadrant of the room. The women were talking about crochet and quilting for awhile.

Suddenly the man, Tye, raised his voice to the supervisor. "Don! Please…talk MAN talk to me!"

Guess Tye found out how women have felt over years of listening conversations about sports, hunting and cars.

* * * * *

My 25 year class reunion occurred in 1998. I made the trip back to Indiana for the event which took place at a restaurant on the grounds of the Indianapolis Museum of Art. I'd gone to a small Catholic high school so my graduating class had only 50 students – all girls.

About 36 of them came to the dinner and they could bring their husbands. After eating there was a large room with a dance floor and music where the women mostly sat around talking and catching up on the last 25 years. Their husbands wandered around, or sat at the bar. Some of them knew each other through associations with their spouse's friends.

We had a program with all the classmates' names, addresses and current occupations listed. The fact that I'd made the trip all the way from New Mexico and that I was an Air Traffic Control Specialist caused quite a bit of comment and admiration.

I walked over to the bar to get a drink and take it back to where I was enjoying a conversation with old friends. As I stood there a group of five big guys swaggered up and surrounded me.

One of them taunted, "Hey, tell the truth, don't men make better air traffic controllers than women?"

Stress is Relative!

This was one time I actually thought of the exact right thing to say. Keeping my cool I looked directly at him, raised my head and said, "Women handle the stress better." Then I pushed my way by them and rejoined my friends.

To this day I do not know which of my unfortunate classmates was married to that jackass or his buddies, but I feel sorry for them.

* * * * *

It is gratifying to see women becoming more interested in aviation careers. I have noticed more female voices on the radios and several support organizations, such as Women in Aviation International came into being.

I heard a story about two women who worked a tower up in Minnesota who happened to be sisters. One of them had a son about age 6. During a family event, someone asked the son if he was going to be an air traffic controller like his mom.

He responded, "Oh, NO! That's women's work!"

* * * * *

During this time period the FAA offered an opportunity to several people in Flight Service to transition back to Center work. Since I had progressed quite far along that career path before becoming medically disqualified I was one of them.

I thought about it hard, I was now fully recovered physically and had my aviation medical certification back.

Center controllers made a lot more money than Flight Service, and I would be able to stay in Albuquerque. It meant going through Center OJT training again, but I didn't see that as a problem.

What it came down to is money versus happiness. I liked Flight Service and was very comfortable in the job. I made a good salary –

Stress is Relative!

enough to live in a good neighborhood and have some discretionary income. More money would be nice…but not necessary.

In the end I decided not to go back to the Center. Flight Service people talk to pilots while Center and Tower order them around. I had made friends with some of the pilots who would come to the building for their Pilot Briefings and joined a few pilot organizations as an associate member. I loved going up for flights in their small aircraft.

Life Lesson: Don't let money dictate your happiness.

Stress is Relative!

CHAPTER 31

9/11/2001

The entire Air Traffic Control system, and aviation community was rocked by events on the day terrorists flew two aircraft into the World Trade Center, and another one into the Pentagon. A message flashed to every facility around the country – LAND ALL AIRCRAFT IMMEDIATELY.

Over 4,500 aircraft were aloft when that command was issued. Luckily the weather was good over most of the country, but it still took hours to get them all down and parked somewhere, anywhere. The Centers had to look for airports capable of handling the various types of aircraft...you can't land a B747 at any airport with a runway less than a mile and a half long!

Most people were aware that the air carriers were grounded – many of them far from their destinations, many of them outside the borders of the United States. We heard about those people and their experience through mass media. But the order included everything that was in flight – corporate jets, small general aviation aircraft, helicopters, hot air balloons, gliders, and ultralights.

Stress is Relative!

* * * * *

That morning I was sleeping after a midnight shift when my daughter, Melissa, woke me and had me turn on the television. Like everyone else in the U.S. I was stunned by the willful devastation.

The first few hours were crazy as controllers in the ARTCC and Towers directed thousands of aircraft to land. The military closed the borders, so hundreds of people were forced to land outside the country.

After that, the ARTCC and Tower personnel had little to do as only military, law enforcement and emergency aircraft were allowed to fly for a couple weeks.

During this time Flight Service took thousands of calls hourly from pilots who only had one question: "When can we fly?"

Over the ensuing weeks the FAA allowed aircraft to take to the air in stages. Of course all emergency aircraft and the military were still airborne. After a couple days the first civilian group to be given a green light was the agricultural field spraying aircraft. The USDA implored the FAA to allow them to continue this time critical action.

Unfortunately as soon as the general public saw these low altitude craft spraying chemicals over the area they started calling in a panic. "Terrorists are spraying poisons!"

After a week the air carriers were given permission to resume flights, followed by the other corporate and shipping entities. After two weeks general aviation within the country was almost back to normal, but any aircraft caught outside U.S. airspace wanting to come in was still blocked whether they were American citizens or not. With heavy military patrols along the Air Defense Identification Zone, nobody wanted to risk trying to get home under the radar! It took at least five weeks before the system approached normal conditions.

* * * * *

Stress is Relative!

In the aftermath of 9/11 most civilians noted those changes to air travel which involved them personally – heightened security procedures at airports, and less access to flight crews.

The long term repercussions to Air Traffic involved heavier security at all ATC facilities, the creation of new restricted airspaces and new procedures in heavily flown areas.

In the past pilots could call an ATC facility and easily arrange tours for themselves, school groups, student pilots and families. Now all visitors to an ATC facility must give names and personal identification information of all who wish a tour several weeks in advance so they could be approved.

Stress is Relative!

Photo by Dennis Livesay

Stress is Relative!

All hot air balloon photos by Dennis Livesay
Former ABQ AFSS Deputy Manager

Stress is Relative!

CHAPTER 32

The Albuquerque International Balloon Fiesta

Albuquerque has a unique geographical advantage for Hot Air Balloons. The city lies in the Rio Grande valley between a range of dormant volcanoes to the west and the Sandia Mountains to the east. The standard wind flow from the west strikes the face of the mountain and bounces back and forth setting up what is known as the "Albuquerque Box" effect.

In most places when balloonists takes off, they are at the mercy of the winds – so the crews on the ground, the "chasers", are driving their pickup trucks erratically on whatever roads they can find in pursuit of their balloons. The Box effect allows the pilot to take off and ascend to an altitude that pushes the balloon south initially. Lighting the burners and ascending another five hundred feet causes the balloon to hover, a little higher and the wind now comes out of the south and pushes the balloon back to the north.

Stress is Relative!

This means the chasers can wave farewell and take off to go to breakfast knowing that the balloon will be back in the area it departed within a couple hours. As a result it is a popular place for balloonists – and the home of the Albuquerque International Balloon Fiesta.

Since this week long event brings in thousands of people from around the world, the FAA began a practice of placing preflight briefers on the Fiesta grounds so pilots can see the weather charts and have access to all the data they need. Every year ABQ Flight Service would provide the staffing for the event – and it was a popular posting.

Most of the briefings were done in the extreme early morning hours (Balloons fly best in the cool of dawn and are usually back on the ground by about 11am).

* * * * *

Rose in the cramped briefing room during the Balloon Fiesta's Gas Balloon Race working the midnight shift

One event required a flight service specialist to be on duty and available 24 hours. The America's Challenge gas balloon flight would take off from the field in the evening as things cooled down. These helium or hydrogen filled balloons could fly much higher than the hot air balloons – frequently flying over mountains.

The event was simple. The balloons had to take off and stay airborne, riding the winds, as long as possible and as far as possible. The one going the longest distance before landing won the event.

These balloons rose high enough to enter controlled airspace, so each of them was required to carry a transponder which broadcast a predetermined code. The code numbers were given to all the ATC facilities in the nation before the flight began. When ATC radar picked up the code, the altitude and position information relative to the balloon would show up on their scopes so ATC could route aircraft around them.

Gas Balloons lift off after sundown at the Balloon Fiesta

The Flight Service weather briefers had a small room located in the Gas Balloon Challenge Trailer with a dedicated phone line and computers that were set up with weather sites. The pilots or their chase crews would call in and give their positions to the Balloon Fiesta staff, many would ask to speak to a Briefer for updated weather information.

Stress is Relative!

Although many of the balloons landed within 48 hours, some would stay aloft for four or five days. It was fun to look at the computers and charts depicting the location of the various balloons.

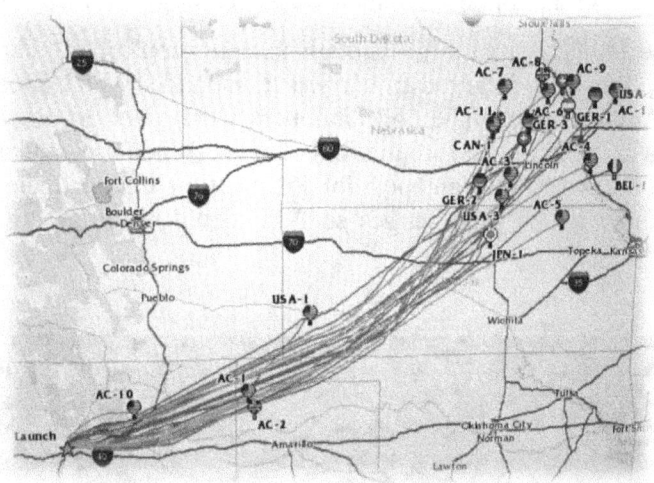

The computer track of Gas balloons after they lifted off from Albuquerque. Competitors come from all over the world.

* * * * *

My responsibilities included keeping track of weather and wind flow across the nation. A few hundred feet of altitude could take the balloons in vastly different directions.

The balloons could not add any more during the flight and were not allowed to land at any time to refuel. (or take potty breaks – but we won't go there) The only way to change altitudes was to let out some gas to descend or toss weight in the form of sandbags out of the basket to go up.

One year there were thunderstorms in the Texas panhandle. One of the crews called to give a position report and wanted wind information.

Stress is Relative!

The RADAR Velocity Azimuth display was showing that winds at 6,000 feet were tracking directly to the storm, but at 8,000 feet they were pushing in a more southeasterly direction. The balloonist emptied a few sandbags and ascended to 8,000. He made it around the storm cell.

* * * * *

In 2001 the Balloon Fiesta was held one month after 9/11. The nation as a whole was both frightened and angry. The first morning after the gas balloons took flight we received a call from a team in western Oklahoma. One of them had been emptying sandbags to gain altitude and heard shooting. There were guys on a pickup truck down on the plains shooting at them!

The sheriff went out and found the pickup truck with several guys who had rifles. They told the Sheriff that there were terrorists pouring poison into our atmosphere.

Once I came on duty for the midnight shift in the Gas Balloon Challenge Center after the race had been going on for four days. All the balloons had landed in various states but for two. Those were over 1200 miles away on widely different tracks. One was heading northeast over Lake Michigan, one was in West Virginia heading directly for Washington D.C.

As the night progressed the Gas Balloon Challenge team was on the phone to the coast guard in the Great Lakes area, and the Canadian authorities about the one, and as for the other….

Let's just say that the airspace around Washington D.C. in the years following 9/11 was bristling with potential disaster. The team was in contact with the secret service and the military and I was on the phone to the air traffic control centers advising them that the transponder target drifting towards the nation's capital was not a threat.

What upped the situation was that the two men on board the balloon drifting towards DC were highly prominent. One was arguably the

Stress is Relative!

world's most renowned balloonist Richard Abruzzo, and the other was a past governor of New Mexico, Gary Johnson – who would go on to run for President of the United States in 2016.

By the next day both balloons had landed. The Canadian Mounties were able to locate the one which landed in the forests north of Lake Michigan. The other managed to skim just south of the restricted airspace around DC and land on an island off the coast of Virginia.

Stress is Relative!

CHAPTER 33

Not Exactly Shakespeare

It was during this period in my life that I began writing professionally. I have been an avid reader since childhood – when I would get sick my Mom did not sit me down in front of a TV, she handed us a book. By the age of eleven I was using her adult pass at the library because the stuff in the kids section was boring and way too easy.

I had been editing and writing little items for various newsletters at my job and for some of the volunteer activities I was involved with, but wanted to expand beyond that. I found a group, the SouthWest Writers (no that is not a typo, they do have a capital in the middle of the name), which meets in Albuquerque twice a month.

Wow! What a fabulous group of people! The whole organization has about 400 members – authors, editors, publishers etc. Each meeting has about 100 in attendance.

My first day there, sitting anonymously in the crowd, I was prepared to just look them over, see what the group was all about. That lasted all of 10 minutes. One of their first orders of business is to ask any visitors or new members to stand up and tell everyone what they write about.

Stress is Relative!

When I stood up I said I wasn't sure exactly what direction to go with my writing, and then mentioned interests in environmental activities and my career in Air Traffic. Wouldn't you know there was a man in the group who was a newsletter editor for the Albuquerque chapter of the Experimental Aircraft Association (EAA).

Jack Hickman (left) introduced himself during the break and asked me if I'd write an article pertaining to preflight briefing for his publication. I figured that would be pretty easy – and sent off a thousand word article that week.

It was published in the local newsletter, and within a week I had requests to publish it in several other chapter newsletters in five states!

The week after that the editor of *America's Flyways*, a national magazine, called and asked if HE could use it. He liked it enough that he asked me to do a monthly column. Over the next couple of years I was asked to write columns for several other magazines and at one point I figured the combined circulation reached a quarter million pilots!

This is where Center, Tower/Approach and Flight Service. The various official FAA documents tell pilots what to do, but not why. My articles cover why and they show the pilots how their actions fit into the big picture.

The extra training I received from the National Weather Service to become Flight Watch certified gave me more insights into regional weather system variations and microclimatology. These are not only useful in general aviation, but also to balloonists, gliders, unmanned air vehicles and even gardeners and concrete workers

Stress is Relative!

Because I write on topics directly connected to my job I was a tad concerned up front about legalities – so I contacted a lawyer specializing in copy write laws. She told me as long as I did not include anything that would be considered proprietary to my employer I could write on pretty much any topic without their permission.

Nonetheless, I made sure that the FAA and later Lockheed Martin were both well aware of my literary activities. I have learned over time that no one, especially employers, like to be surprised.

My articles garnered a good deal of attention from the pilot community and I began receiving requests to speak for various aviation events, including the Balloon Fiesta's Pilot Safety program.

That just goes to show you that no training is ever wasted – I might not be performing onstage in local theaters anymore, but I can still put on a good show!

Rose giving a presentation on Aviation weather to the AAAA Pilots Association during the Albuquerque International Balloon Fiesta.

Stress is Relative!

Melissa (Missy) , Rose and Carolyn (Carrie) circa 1991

Stress is Relative!

CHAPTER 34

Privatization

Flight Service remained a very stable government post for decades. The leaps in technology allowing the consolidation of small facilities into large ones reduced the need for personnel, but in all cases the FAA allowed anyone who wanted to stay employed the option of moving.

As a result, Flight Service was overstaffed for about a decade. Rather than kicking people out of a job the FAA was depending on natural attrition through retirements to reduce the workforce. No new people were brought into the job - which is why I stayed in the bottom third of the seniority list for the first fifteen years of my career.

Flight Service specialists were represented by a different union than the Center and Tower folks. The National Association of Air Traffic Specialists or NAATS was the entity who annually argued with the FAA over our pay and working conditions.

Joining the union was voluntary, but whether you were a paying member or not, they were the ones who negotiated our pay and working conditions with the FAA.

Technology was rapidly taking over many of the Flight Service duties – further reducing the FAA's need to maintain so large a workforce. On top of that, the long term government reforms and labor laws were ensuring the basic needs of employees in terms of working conditions and pay were fair and equitable.

The Bush (Jr) administration aggressively began looking for federal government divisions to privatize. In 2003 the FAA announced they were commissioning a study to determine if Flight Service and some Air Traffic Control Towers could be successfully managed by a private corporation.

That was scary. Government service is usually a nice safe post, no matter what division you are in. You had to screw up big time to get fired, because most of the time the U.S. Government gamely tried to rehabilitate you. The only things that could flat out get you fired were striking a fellow employee, breaking a law, deliberately harassing someone or falsifying government records. If you messed up at work – even repeatedly – you wouldn't normally be fired, though you might be reassigned.

Now all of a sudden everyone was uncertain of their future. They weren't so much afraid that a new company coming in would immediately fire them and hire new people at lower salaries – the length of time it takes to train someone to do the job precluded that.

Going to a new company would mean that all the salaries, benefits and working conditions currently in effect could be stripped away. The Union's contract was with the federal government. Once the managing corporation took over, the Union would no longer have any power until and unless the workforce held a vote to re-unionize.

Who knows what kind of treatment to expect from a large corporate entity?

The study lasted over a year. Then the FAA formally announced it was going to privatize Flight Service and the bid was released. We heard that several companies were interested. Whenever anyone heard of a new one we looked them up on the internet.

The Harris Corporation, who had developed the Oasis software we currently used, decided to join up with a division of the FAA (don't ask me how that worked) and put in a bid. The Union was totally behind that one, because they would remain in power, and right up to the day the winners of the bid were announced the Union rep in our facility was telling us that the Harris/FAA bid was a sure thing.

The bids closed in March of 2005 and it was announced that as of October 4, 2005 the Lockheed Martin Corporation would take over management of Flight Service.

Suddenly everyone was faced with making major decisions. The workforce was old enough that a third of them could retire from the FAA and jump over to Lockheed immediately – for that group the change was good – they could begin receiving funds from their retirement accounts and still be employed.

Some were just a few weeks, months or years from that happy situation – these people began searching frantically for a way to stay employed by the government long enough to attain the minimum time needed.

The rest of the specialists were still pretty far from retirement, so switching to a new employer would neither help nor hinder them. However there was another facet to consider. As part of the contract Lockheed Martin was required to continue the practice of closing and consolidating sites.

On the day they took control, there were 58 Flight Service facilities in the lower 49 United States – almost half were closed in 2007, and most of the rest in 2008. As of 2013 there were only three major Flight Service Hub facilities and two smaller support facilities left south of Alaska. (Alaska is still under FAA management as of the time of this publication)

I was one of those who was ALMOST to retirement age. In air traffic, as long as you work in the operations areas you are getting "good time", when you move into management you are still accumulating time but the rules change.

Retirement from air traffic control is accomplished one of two ways: 20 years of active operational service "Good Time" and age 50, or 25 years of active service at any age.

Stress is Relative!

I had 23.5 years of "good time" on the date the government terminated our employment and turned us over to Lockheed – October 3, 2005. But my 50th birthday was October 4th – the next day.

At first the government made noises about us not being able to apply our leave balances to get to retirement, but the National Labor Laws allowed anyone who had leave available to use it to get to that date if it was within reach. (Whew!)

For others, a U.S. Senator from Maine, Olympia J. Snowe initiated a bill which allowed displaced federal employees who were within two years of retirement to remain on the federal payroll while working for the new contractor so they could qualify for retirement and health insurance benefits.

Nonetheless, many people who were not allowed to transfer to another FAA job and had to settle for a reduced annuity were angry and initiated a lawsuit that is still not settled.

For weeks before the changeover, some employees jumped into other FAA or federal government jobs, so by October 4th the number of people working at some facilities was lessened by 15 to 20%. Other than that the actual switchover was pretty transparent. One day we worked for the Federal Government, the next day we did the same thing in the same location but our paycheck was signed by Lockheed Martin.

To sweeten the deal with the FAA, Lockheed had agreed to allow those employees who came over to keep their pay levels and leave benefits. They called it the "Soft Landing Package". New employees coming in would have to adhere to Lockheed corporate policies, but those who transitioned in from the FAA would see little difference.

Stress is Relative!

CHAPTER 35

Lockheed Martin Flight Service

The day Lockheed Martin took over administration of the Flight Service division saw few changes to the actual job functions. We worked the same job, in the same place under the same managers on October 4th, 2005 that we did on October 3rd.

The night before, the two guys working the midnight shift decided to greet the morning shift wearing tuxedos. They told everyone it was the new dress code.

The facility secretary brought in a planter with a card from the Vice President of Lockheed Martin who oversaw our program welcoming all of us to the company.

The only significant changes were that we were now paid weekly instead of bi-weekly and NAATS – the Flight Service union -no longer existed except in Alaska.

Lockheed did not make any changes for a few months – all the managers, supervisors and staff people as well as specialists continued doing what they had always done. During that time Lockheed monitored and assessed the managers who were in place and as opportunities arose there were many new positions created.

Stress is Relative!

Lockheed Martin won the Flight Service contract, but they were not really prepared for it.

To be fair, the FAA had not really briefed those companies who were bidding on the contract on every aspect of what was required. Like all the other bidders, Lockheed had hired "experts" – former flight service managers most of whom had retired many years earlier and had no idea of the level of technical sophistication which had been achieved and probably had not worked in the operations area for 20 years!

The bidding companies were not allowed to go to flight service stations and take notes or see what and how we did our jobs. They were given a contract and access to the FAA's governing document for Flight Service, FAA Order 7110.10 – which did not cover all aspects of the job.

At first all Lockheed asked of the facilities was to continue operations as normal – except that there were services performed by FSS which were not covered under the contract. The most critical one was the issuance of Notices to Airmen or NOTAMs.

As of midnight October 4th, flight service specialists were instructed to no longer take calls from airport managers or other aviation professionals who wanted to issue NOTAMs.

Since at that time FSS was the primary input agent for much of this data, the US NOTAM office (USNO) had a fit, as did a few hundred airport managers. With hundreds of phone calls inundating the USNO, the FAA quickly discovered their error and by the end of the first week the contract with Lockheed was adjusted to include that responsibility.

Stress is Relative!

* * * * *

Another part of the contract concerned the computer programs and equipment Lockheed was required to produce to replace the OASIS and M1FC programs all around the country. Again, the decision to employ retired managers whose knowledge of the current level of technology being used at flight service hampered development.

In the operations area things were changing daily. Now that there was a contract, there were clauses in the contract which indicated that if the FAA ascertained that Flight Service was not performing according to the handbook then they could financially penalize the company.

For decades the specialists had been doing the job to the satisfaction of the FAA, but all of a sudden the FAA was scrutinizing them in a far more detailed manner than had been done by the in house FAA Quality Assurance staff. Saying one word wrong in a 15 minute briefing or a radio call would be a "failure" of a performance measurement. Only a small number of failures were allowed before penalties were assessed.

It took years for the FAA and Lockheed to hammer out what actually constituted a failure for any given service, versus what was simply a phraseology error. But during those first days the facility managers were under a lot of pressure to make everything we did perfect.

Many of the Flight Service managers had never really had any management training. It appeared to the workforce that many were promoted based on seniority and in some cases favoritism.

Once Lockheed took over the NAATS union contract was abolished, so facility managers were faced with making decisions which affected work schedules, leave, and many other topics.

In our facility the manager suddenly told everyone they were going to have to change their work shifts – everyone would be required to work two evenings, two days and either a midnight shift or very early morning shift every week. This type of work schedule was called a rattler and it

Stress is Relative!

was extremely hard on a workforce that was accustomed to being assigned either all evenings, all days or midnights.

Everyone protested but the manager told us "You don't like it you can go and get another job." He would not allow us to trade shifts with each other. He told us the schedule change was mandated by Lockheed.

The physical disruption caused by this action manifested across everyone in the facility within weeks. After three of our employees went to the emergency room with stress related disorders, I went to him and asked if he had any objection to my sending a letter to the Human Relations Manager about the problems this schedule was causing. He looked at me and growled, "I don't care what you do."

So I did. I wrote the letter and sent it certified mail and gave our manager a copy so he would know what was said.

Lockheed's Human Relations Manager called me at home the next day and asked questions. "He won't even let you trade shifts with each other?" he asked.

I told him we had been told that Lockheed insisted the employees had to work this schedule. He responded, "No, the managers were simply told to be fair."

Apparently our manager figured that "Fair" meant we all had to work the same number of aircraft and that meant we had to rotate shifts.

Within 48 hours my supervisor was walking around and asked the specialists what kind of shift they would prefer.

* * * * *

How did the manager respond? Not well. In his eyes I had made him look bad. He couldn't do anything overtly, but he asked the quality assurance staff member to assess my performance.

Stress is Relative!

A few weeks later I was called into his office with a supervisor present. He played an audio tape of me working the Flight Watch position and had some graphics showing the weather conditions at the time.

I spoke to a pilot in northern Arizona headed to Grand Junction, Colorado VFR. After giving him the AIRMETs for IFR and Mountain obscuration, I told him that these advisories were old and soon to be updated, and that the current conditions and satellites indicated the low cloud activity had already dissipated. Just to be on the safe side I asked him if he did encounter low clouds could he go IFR? He said yes, so I gave him an altimeter setting and ended the call.

After listening, the manager asked me what I thought of it. I said it sounded like I did well according to the rules we worked by.

He exploded.

One of the statements that flight service specialists are supposed to make when a VFR pilot is flying into low clouds or AIRMETS for low clouds is "VFR NOT RECOMMENDED". But the handbook also says that the statement is not compulsory in all situations, and in this case I had already determined it was not a factor as the clouds had burned off.

But the manager used it as an excuse to scream at me so hard that as he rose up from his chair and leaned across his desk there was spit flying into my face. He told me that the pilot SHOULD have crashed and if he had crashed it would be my fault for not saying "VFR not recommended."

Did I get upset? Not really. His actions were so over the top that I had a hard time believing it was happening so I was able to sit back and quietly ask him, "So what happens now?"

After sulking a few minutes he said "I'll tell you your punishment tomorrow."

Punishment? Was I suddenly back in grade school?

* * * * *

Stress is Relative!

When I thought about the interview later, I think he was actually trying to make me react physically in some way that would allow him to fire me. It was unfortunate for him that I am a woman. Most men get angry when they are treated that way, some women cry when they are angry. I had already had loads of crap flung at me in my early years with the FAA and so I simply stared at him quietly until he said I was dismissed to go back to work.

Two days later my supervisor came and gave me a letter of reprimand signed by the manager and told me I had to sit in the back room and read through the Flight Watch section of the flight service handbook. I was on an evening shift, so as soon as the manager left the building, my supervisor (who was ashamed to be in the position of disciplining someone he thought wronged) called me out of the back and put me on position as usual.

I was not the only one to receive this kind of treatment. The manager was heard ranting at many specialists and supervisors for minor infractions blown out of proportion. One of them, upon being notified he had to go see the manager for the second time, stood up, handed the supervisor on duty his headset, cleared out his locker and quit.

The manager of our facility was not the only one whose actions were dramatically affecting his employees. Lockheed began firing those managers whose actions proved their incompetence – he was one of them.

To be fair, our manager was a good man at heart. As long as he only had to walk the tightrope between FAA regulations and Union contract requirements he was very easy to get along with and pretty much sat in his office doing the paperwork while the supervisors handled operations. He'd had a good rapport with the union representative and the place ran so smoothly we'd received the FAA's highest honor "Flight Service Station of the Year".

Once the union was ousted he wasn't sure what to do. Lockheed is adamant that failures in a facility are put on the managers shoulders and the whole new world of contract performance penalties for "failures" was daunting. Everyone was doing the same job in the same way we had done it for decades – with much closer oversight.

Stress is Relative!

* * * * *

The manager's replacement, Steve, was a congenial man who had come from a management background. Suddenly you could request leave and be given an answer with enough time to arrange travel again, and supervisors could discuss performance shortcomings with their people without the manager dictating every move.

One positive change Lockheed Martin made was to initiate a three step system for specialists which it was hoped would create a more define pathway into management based on ability rather than seniority. Wow! What a concept.

Lockheed knew that the workforce primarily consisted of older people who could choose to retire, so they created an Academy of their own at the Prescott Flight Service Hub and began hiring new specialists.

Level 1 specialists were the new trainees. They had to complete training and spend some time in operations before they could be promoted to Level 2. The men and women who came over from the FAA were automatically Level 2, but then Lockheed created a Level 3 position with a pay raise that was halfway between specialist and supervisor.

I bid on one of the Level 3's, though I was concerned that the Letter of Reprimand the former manager gave me might quash that hope. But as it turned out, he never filed a copy of the letter in the facility or sent it to the higher ups in the organization as managers were supposed to do. For that matter, he had been issuing a lot of letters of reprimand without obtaining permission to do so, or filing them.

With that removed as a hindrance my record was unblemished. I was promoted into a Level 3 and was there a year more before Lockheed announced they were closing Albuquerque Flight Service.

Stress is Relative!

CHAPTER 36

End of an Era for ABQ AFSS

The announcement that Albuquerque Flight Service was closing came about two years before anyone expected it. Before the changeover from FAA to LMCO, we were told by corporate managers that there were no plans to close this facility before 2010. Many people were basing retirement options on that information. We learned that "There are no plans to close", is a very imprecise statement. They had no plans to close it that day…but they may have plans to close it as of the next day.

Everyone at ABQ who was not quite ready for retirement went scrambling to find a berth somewhere else. Suddenly everything that had been stable and settled in our lives turned upside down. We got the word the first of October 2007 that ABQ would be shut down in January.

My husband and I fell into the category of not yet ready to retire and though we both had degrees which would allow us to look for other jobs in the workforce, we agreed that nothing else would pay as well at this point in time. We had kids in college and other debts to pay off.

In the end we decided to continue employment with Flight Service if we could find positions at one of the large Hub facilities and two of our kids became house sitters. The beautiful mountains and sunsets, the wonderful dry climate and fascinating mixture of cultures had become part of us, so we knew we would eventually come home to Albuquerque.

Stress is Relative!

* * * * *

As all the smaller facilities closed, specialists could bid on positions in one of the three Hubs which would eventually be the only Flight Service Stations left in the country. These were located at Washington, D.C. (DCA), Fort Worth, Texas (FTW) and Prescott, AZ (PRC).

The Hub facility in Prescott, Arizona was our first choice, but its manager preferred to hire specialists from facilities west of a line from Arizona to Montana at this time. We did not want to live in Fort Worth, which left only one possibility, the Washington D.C. Hub located in Ashburn, Virginia (DCA). We put in our bids thinking that we could go to DCA and eventually work our way back west to Prescott as openings became available.

The East Coast is not and was not my concept of a comfortable living environment. I had grown to despise humidity – and here we were about to move to reclaimed swamp land.

My husband and I were accepted at DCA and flew out to check out housing a month before the transition date. We found a one bedroom apartment in Ashburn that was only six miles from the DCA facility – with a monthly rent that was higher than the mortgage on our house!

* * * * *

We continued working at ABQ AFSS until the day it closed. By that time there were about 34 people left, and all of us met for dinner at the Black Angus Steakhouse that night.

I'm not going to say that everybody always got along with everyone, or that there were not people that were just royal pains to work with, but in general the folks at ABQ were a really good bunch. The ones who'd survived the transition to Lockheed had become pretty close as we all learned how to jump through corporate hoops and still satisfy the FAA requirements we'd honored for decades.

For several years thereafter, one of the guys organized a monthly brunch at a local restaurant. I would join in if I happened to be in town,

Stress is Relative!

and since we always came back for the International Balloon Fiesta, we would host a party for everybody at our house during that week.

Friends we made there are still friends today, and we love to get together with them and their families whenever possible. We were the only two who were going to DCA. Several others transitioned to Fort Worth and three of them did make it into the Prescott Hub. Many chose to retire and stay in Albuquerque.

That is the nature of Air Traffic Control, whenever you transition to a new facility you will meet people from all around the country.

* * * *

Stress is Relative!

CHAPTER 37

Washington Flight Service (DCA)

We moved in January of 2008 in the aftermath of an ice storm. The Washington Hub was considerably larger than Albuquerque with over ten times as many employees! This Hub was set up to take pilot's radio and phone calls throughout the eastern third of the country.

My career at the DCA Hub commenced with huge success. Lockheed Martin annually gave awards to specialist's whose work performance was outstanding. The day I showed up at the DCA Hub I was in a classroom studying my new area and the trainer told me I was wanted on the Bridge.

The Bridge is what we call the raised dais in the center of a large operations room where supervisors can monitor everyone at their workstations. I walked up and saw that the facility chief, and the national chief, as well as a lot of staff members were present.

You can imagine my surprise when they announced to everyone present that I was receiving the National Flight Service Specialist of the Year award for 2007!

Wow!

My previous station chief who had moved to Fort Worth after Albuquerque closed, was listening in via Telcon. He knew about it but had kept quiet, so the surprise was complete.

What a way to start out in a new facility!

Stress is Relative!

* * * * *

By now many of the smaller Flight Service facilities across the nation had closed. Over time, the ones that were left primarily performed only Preflight functions with the other services being handled by the Hubs.

All the Flight Data services including Search and Rescue, communications with ATC, Airport managers, and all the Radio communications with airborne pilots were centralized regionally. As of the time of this writing, there is only one smaller facility left open for preflight briefing and flight plan filing support.

Each of the major Hubs served about a third of the country. The DCA Hub handled everything east of the Mississippi. The Central part of the country belonged to a facility in Fort Worth (FTW), and the western third was served by the Hub in Prescott Valley, Arizona (PRC).

The specialists working in the Hubs are assigned "areas of responsibility" (AOR). Over 100 consoles on the operations floor were divided into 4 sectors, with each sector handling several states. I was assigned to the Great Lakes Region covering the states of Ohio, Michigan, Indiana, Illinois and Wisconsin.

Once I finished learning the Great Lakes area knowledge package I started training out in operations and was certified within a month. The basic procedures, rules and phraseology had been part of my psyche since the Academy days. I just needed to learn the weather, terrain, charts and airports in my new area. It helped that I'd grown up in the Midwest and knew most of the geography and place names.

Most of the specialists working there transferred in when their previous facilities had closed, and the majority were working the territory which previously was served by their former facilities.

I retained my Level 3 status, which meant I had additional responsibilities. This meant assisting the supervisors with overseeing the operations floor and performing On-the-Job Training (OJT) instruction.

Stress is Relative!

The DCA Hub was located in Ashburn, Virginia – just 30 miles west of Washington D.C. It was not close to any airport, but the proximity allowed Senate and Congress people overseeing the FAA's contracts to visit the facility on occasion.

* * * * *

After about five months a position opened up on the Quality Assurance (QA) staff. My husband encouraged me to apply, though by that time I was very comfortable in my current job. Nonetheless, I tossed my hat in the ring and (surprise!) was awarded the position.

This was a major turning point in my career, my first management level job. For the first time I had the chance to listen to a different perspective on the overall running of an ATC facility.

As a specialist I had been required to perform my duties in such a way as to meet the expectations of the FAA. As a QA I was still expected to maintain my operational skills which gave me credibility when it came to analyzing the work performance of others.

Each element of the job was scrutinized using procedures hammered out in the FAA contract. Lockheed Martin had its QA team and the FAA had a similar team made up of former Flight Service specialists. Every month the LMCO QA team monitored analyzed and scored a set number of services. The FAA team reviewed our findings to make sure we were scoring fairly and abiding by the contract.

Each QA team member had a specialty, and I was assigned to monitor the Inflight/Radio position. I learned how to access the recordings and gather pertinent data, then enter my findings into the system.

The DCA QA team had four women and five men. In addition to the monthly service analysis we each contributed skills to the group. Two of the team were computer whizzes, one was a genius at putting together detailed information packages for the FAA.

I had a fabulous boss and mentor, Scott Cunningham, who told me I was the most naturally analytical person he'd ever met. The National

Stress is Relative!

QA manager, Glenn Reffner agreed and both of them contributed to enhancing my success as a Quality Assurance Engineer. Within a year I won a regional award in that department.

Many people reading this memoir will have seen the articles I write for national aviation magazines and pilot newsletters, so they know I enjoy sharing information. Scott gave me a challenge, an assignment to develop a daylong seminar for the engineers who designed and maintained our computer programs which would give them insights into Flight Service responsibilities and compare those responsibilities with the computer programs we were currently using.

The first time the seminar was given, the engineers came up with over a 135 ideas for tweaking the programs to make the job more efficient. For that I received my second National Award, though the bosses were sneaky about how it was presented.

A couple months earlier I'd been tasked to do an analysis of whether a certain computer program (HIWAS) was functioning correctly and then present my findings to an FAA committee downtown. One day Scott told me I was wanted in the office of the national manager of Flight Service, Jim Derr, and to bring my HIWAS notes.

Quickly I grabbed my folder and followed him to the other side of the building. There was a crowd of people by Derr's office but Scott pushed through them with me tagging along behind him.

We were standing off to the side as Derr was talking with several other department heads. Derr saw me and said, "Ahh, Rose! Come over here."

I was expecting him to ask me something about the HIWAS analysis, but instead he said "A month ago you gave a presentation to 34 engineers about Flight Service…"

Derr went on to describe the impact my class had on the Flight Service program in general and the changes it prompted to our computer programs. As he continued, Scott reached over and took the file folders from my hand before I dropped them. My heart started thumping and I think I flushed from my toes to the crown of my head.

Stress is Relative!

Suddenly I realized that all those department heads were there to honor ME!

Derr handed me a lovely plaque signed by himself and several of the other department heads. I thanked him and told them all I enjoyed doing it, but I was so stunned I couldn't think of anything else to say.

Scott said he never saw anyone turn bright red so fast. I never saw that one coming!

* * * * *

Rose giving a tour to a pilot group visiting the DCA AFSS

One of the problems employees had with the DCA hub was its location. It sits in Loudoun County, Virginia – which has the highest per capita income in the United States. There are huge mansions and the roadways and malls all have color coordinated landscaping. It also means that apartment rentals and property values are sky high.

216

Stress is Relative!

Almost half of the people working at DCA did not live anywhere near the facility. Many of them lived over 45 minutes away in West Virginia or Maryland.

We'd brought two vehicles with us – one of them was a GMC Sierra one ton pickup with dual rear tires. The dually made us the butt of more than a few jokes initially in this "sophisticated" environment. We could not even BEGIN to take it into downtown D.C. – it would easily fill two parking spaces.

They all stopped laughing when "Snow-mageddeon" hit the area. Five feet of snow fell in 36 hours. Everything was closed, government offices, subways, restaurants, stores – the plows could not keep up.

Flight Service is a 24/7 responsibility but many people could not get to work….or go home if they were at work. Facility management, knowing the storm was coming, had purchased and set up a room full of cots for those who were stuck there. One of the managers, Frank Preston brought in food and made breakfast. (Frank was a navy chef and a WONDERFUL cook!)

My husband and his dually helped some of the locals get to and from work and together we loaded up a bunch of food we had at home so I could make a big spaghetti dinner in the Flight Service breakroom. (Growing up in Indiana taught me to always have enough to feed an army stashed away in case of bad weather!)

* * * * *

In addition to the hub staff, the DCA building housed the national management offices for Lockheed Martin Flight Service. My boss's boss and his boss were all in the same building. This allowed a closer interaction in the QA department and we participated in several team building initiatives.

I enjoyed working with the members of my team and occasionally socialized with them outside of work. My boss, Scott, and his wife, Brenda volunteered at an animal rescue ranch about 20 miles west of the facility. It primarily took care of horses which had been abandoned or

Stress is Relative!

abused, though the property also housed goats, pigs, llamas, rabbits and a camel.

Scott invited anyone from the team who wanted to help with the animals to come out to the ranch and exercise the horses. I went along and spent the day singing with a cockatoo, chasing down a baby pig, and brushing horses in addition to going for a ride.

He was amazing with the animals. To help raise money for the facility he would transport a bunch of them (including the camel) to the homes of people for their kid's parties.

Scott and a friend on their way to a fundraising event.

* * * * *

Stress is Relative!

The job was good, the people I worked with were great, but I was not happy living in the Washington D.C. area. My husband and I did all the normal touristy stuff – we visited Mount Vernon, the White House, the senate, the library of congress. We went to a Nationals Baseball game and the ballet at Rockefeller Center. Of course we toured the Smithsonian – several times. It's a really interesting place to visit, but for a girl from the southwest it was not a fun place to live.

As I've mentioned, both of us hate humid environments, and the whole greater D.C. area is built on a swamp. Some days you feel like you can cut the air with a knife. The sweat lays on your skin like saran wrap winter and summer.

We stayed inside a lot more than we had back home and I started writing a book on how to run fundraising events for small to medium Non-Profit groups. Over a 25 year time period I'd volunteered for a lot of organizations from girls scouts and church groups to the NM Solar Energy Association, and had managed quite a few fundraisers.

FUNdraising Events went on the market in 2010. I continued writing my monthly columns on aviation, and occasional pieces for sustainable living magazines.

Stress is Relative!

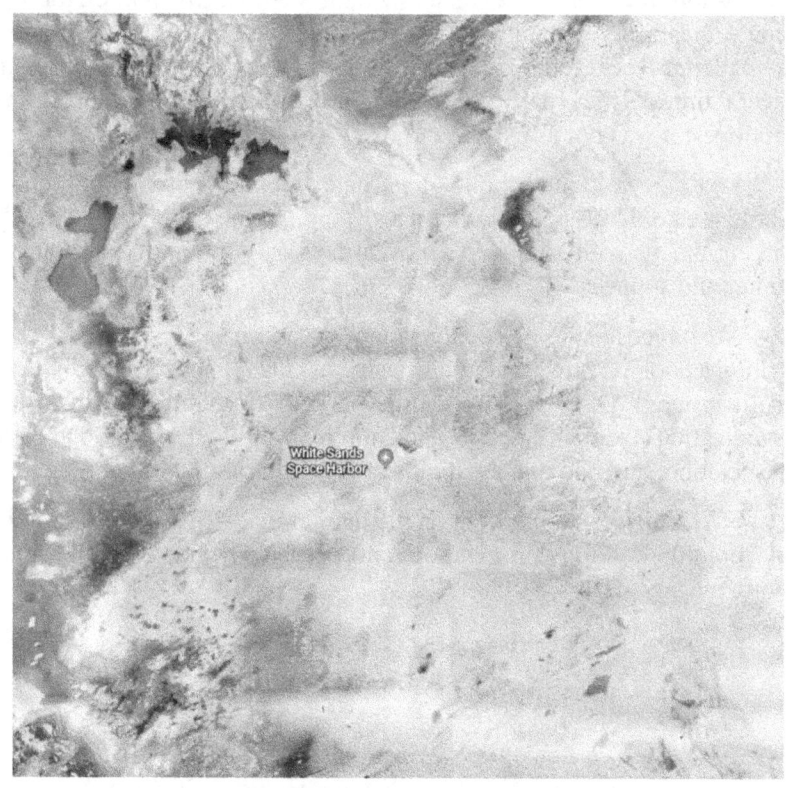

White Sands Space Harbor (WSSH)
From satellite it is very hard to see the
5 mile long gypsum runways!

Stress is Relative!

CHAPTER 38

White Sands Space Harbor

With the desert calling to my soul I kept an eye out for potential jobs in the Southwest. Lockheed managed an Air Traffic Control Tower at White Sands Space Harbor, so when a position came open I bid into it.

What a different world! This airport was built for only one purpose – the Space Shuttle Program. It's location in the center of restricted airspace extending from the surface up to 60,000 feet made it a perfect place for the Shuttle pilots to practice landings, and it was an alternate landing spot in case the Space Shuttle landing gear was broken or weather closed down the coastal facilities.

If you go to *google earth* and focus on south central New Mexico you can see a big white spot – that is White Sands. The National Park is on the east side of the area, the Space Harbor was on the west side.

While working El Paso Flight Service, I had the privilege of flying with the shuttle pilots while they were doing their practice landings at White Sands. Now I was on the other end of the microphone during their exercises!

Two new controllers, myself and a man named Shamseldeen, in-processed at the Johnson Space Center in August of 2010 and were privileged to be given a tour of the grounds. One of the current controllers, Ben, met us and had us drive our own vehicles out to the entry gate, then chauffeured us to our new workplace.

Stress is Relative!

As we drove down the road he pointed out some of the hazards of the region. WSSH (pronounced WISH) is located in the southern end of the White Sands Missile Range, and as its name suggests, the military and research scientists use it to test rockets and bombs.

One of the films we were required to view before working at WSSH instructed us in safety procedures. It showed many kinds of bomb casings. If we saw anything unusual in the roads or areas we worked in, even if it looked like a child's toy, we were to stay WAY back and call a special phone number to report it so that the bomb squad could check it out because sometimes they don't detonate on impact.

OOOOHHHH KKKAAAY!!!

What made it interesting was that whenever there was active testing going on in the range, the entire workforce of the WSSH site was transported over to Holloman Air Force Base.

Bob also pointed out a herd of Oryx on the side of the road. He slowed way down because these are very large animals imported from Asia that were transported to New Mexico because they were on the endangered species list. Few predators could threaten the 450 pound Oryx in their new home so they prospered to the degree that they overpopulated the region and regulated hunting was allowed.

The road wound around the south side of a mountain and emptied out into the large basin containing the huge White Sands area you can see on satellite. We drove by the administrative office building, which is just off the gypsum sand edges, and continued into the heart of the facility. All told we spent two hours every day just driving in and out of the complex from the gate, and six hours on duty.

Stress is Relative!

At the center of the complex is a structure where the controllers and technicians have their desks. Behind it is a facility occupied by emergency personnel and paramedics brought in from Holloman Air Force Base whenever shuttle practice is going on – as a "just in case" measure.

The structure began life as a single wide mobile home set down in the middle of the desert. It was sprayed with a white compound of some kind to make it appear to be a large snowdome from a distance with windows and a carport. The white reflects the sun's intense radiation away from the interior to keep it as cool as possible in summer.

Next to that building is the Control Tower. I have seen some interesting Towers in my time, but this one was unique. A round metal missile launch pad comprised the base with a structure built on top with windows all around. There was a small communications console for talking to other ATC facilities, a couple of old fashioned dial telephones and a small air conditioner.

There were was a radio for talking to aircraft but, no recorders. It had an altimeter and wind readout, some binoculars, note pads and miscellaneous small items littering the console. By ATC standards it was very primitive. You had to climb down the long staircase to visit the restroom inside the office structure.

Handheld walkie talkie type radios were used to communicate with ground vehicles. They were kept in the main structure on chargers whenever they weren't used in the Tower.

Of course there was no janitorial service out there so we all took turns keeping the place picked up and cleaned out. Strong desert winds forced white gypsum dust and sand into every miniscule crack and corner.

The sand is made of gypsum crystals and in the area of the Space Harbor covered an underground aquifer which was very close to the surface. The runways were five miles long - made of compacted gypsum – not asphalt or concrete – so they were very soft. No aircraft were allowed to land there and only the maintenance vehicles were ever allowed anywhere on the airport surface.

All the airport personnel lived either in Las Cruces or Alamogordo. We drove about 35 miles to the entrance gates east of the Organ Pipe Mountains where we parked for the day and took NASA trucks onto the base. From there it was about an hour's drive to the airport. Personal vehicles were not allowed because the gypsum sands are very corrosive.

Earlier I described how the practice aircraft were based in El Paso and how they would go to the space harbor, fly up to 35,000 feet and practice landing – without ever touching the wheels to the surface of the runway – just taking off again when they were at the right visual levels.

I was told that if any of them EVER landed or even touched a wheel to the surface that we were required to declare an emergency.

Over the life of the program only one shuttle ever actually landed at the Space Harbor. The *Columbia* landed because of inclement weather at Edwards Air Force Base, its primary landing site, on March 30, 1982.

Although the aircraft underwent major cleaning efforts, the next time it went into space the astronauts reported a cloud of white dust poofing outside when the cargo bay doors were opened. The shuttle left a trail of gypsum sand for about an orbit and a half.

* * * * *

The shuttle program was winding down with only a couple of space flights left. From the beginning, NASA contracted out the running of White Sands Space Harbor (WSSH) to a firm which kept the airport surface maintained and ready. FAA technicians worked onsite to keep all the lights and navigational equipment working.

That company contracted Lockheed Martin to manage the Air Traffic Control tower. There were four controllers whose primary shifts were day and evening.

Stress is Relative!

Since the only people using the facility for landing practice were the Shuttle Pilots, and the practice runs were set up well in advance, the controllers were also given duties on the airport to accomplish in their down time.

Because they knew the program was ending, the two most senior controllers bid out to other jobs, leaving two vacancies. Lockheed Martin filled those posts with myself and a wonderful man who worked in the Miami Flight Service facility. Shams was a pilot and had a degree in aviation before coming to the job.

Right from the beginning this situation was strange. Shams and I were interviewed over the phone and given our traveling orders. We understood that the situation was temporary, but expected it to last for about 18 months.

* * * * *

The first few days were spent getting our computers set up with security passcodes. Ben drove us up and down the runways and taxiways pointing out the navigational aids and lighting systems. There were no shuttle practices scheduled for that week, so we learned our "other duties".

I was assigned recordkeeping for the airfield fleet of maintenance trucks and vehicles – making sure they were licensed and routinely serviced, as well as monitoring the electricity used onsite by visiting the meters around the airport grounds and entering usage data. I also kept records of rainfall on the airfield – a very easy job.

What was strange was that we were not initially given ANY training materials related to our primary job function. As I've stated before, training normally begins the minute you walk in the door of any new ATC facility.

The main administrative building at the airport had one large breakroom/meeting room surrounded by offices. One of the side rooms contained a rather primitive radar which the controllers on the airport manned in addition to the tower during the Shuttle training practices. It mostly showed the boundaries of Holloman Air Force Base Approach

Stress is Relative!

control to the east and the points over which the NASA pilots reported on their way inbound. There was a phone to the tower and one to Holloman, but not much more and no radios.

* * * * *

In many ways White Sands Space Harbor was an island landlocked by the missile range. Few people worked there, fewer ever visited. The facilities were decades old and with the space shuttle program winding down they were seldom used.

As I mentioned, a different company managed the airport and Lockheed Martin was subcontracted to that company – not directly to NASA. Towards the end of the first week Shams and I met with the Airport/Contract Manager – for now I'll call him Heinrich.

We both sat in the office expecting the usual general corporate-type welcome that new employees are given…but that's not what we got.

Heinrich hemmed and hawed and then he described the general staffing of the airport - who did what – and some of the rules of the place. NO one was allowed to stay on site after hours unless there was a night flight by NASA – and then everyone was required to be there. Those were scheduled way in advance. He mentioned that he had been managing the place since the beginning of the shuttle program.

He kept looking sideways as though he wanted to say something but couldn't figure out how. Then he turned to me and said. "We've had other women try and work out here, but they usually quit within a few days."

He went on. "This is a pretty hot and dry environment, sometimes the septic system gets full or messed up and we have to resort to the outhouses, they can be pretty hot in the summer."

I knew I was the only woman working at the airport. I just smiled and said "No problem, I'm used to the desert – as a matter of fact I own property about 60 miles northeast of here and I have camped in some pretty primitive areas. It won't be a problem."

For some reason, that did not make him happy.

Stress is Relative!

Then he kept looking down, then glancing up at Shams and mentioned, seemingly to both of us, that he won't tolerate any religious types trying to push their beliefs on people. He told us there used to be a guy who wanted to hold prayer meetings at lunch time – he didn't want to see anything like that.

Now, the thing is, Shams was born in Egypt and came to the U.S. as a child. He is an American citizen and practices the Islamic faith. He is a gentleman and very low key. I've had dinner with his family several times and you could not find a better set of people anywhere in the country.

Heinrich made sure to not say anything directly that could get him in trouble legally, but both Shams and I did not exactly feel welcome.

* * * * *

There were only two shuttle launches scheduled over the last 18 months of the program and very few astronauts were making the trip from Houston to practice. They flew during the second week we were there one day. Shams and I were able to sit in the tower and observe the action for a total of two hours.

The next week was devoid of practice flights, but we did have a day where the military wanted to lob bombs around – so instead of driving to the usual gate we took the highway all the way around to Holloman Air Force Base in Alamogordo.

NASA kept a building on site where people could basically hang out whenever they were evacuated from the field – it was small and we were not required to stay there. We could wander around most of the base and use the library, stores and gym. We had the hand held radios so whenever the rockets were done we were either dismissed and sent home or required to go back to the field.

* * * * *

Stress is Relative!

Shams and I were both concerned because there was really no training being done and we brought it up to Bob, who acted as lead controller. The manager for all four of us worked out of a facility in California and did not touch base often. We'd only met him over the phone.

Bob told us we could take the vehicles out anytime the maintenance techs did not need them and wander around the airport to become familiar with it. Most of the time we all ended up sitting at our desks doing little and trying not to be bored.

Shams and I would go for walks out on the taxiways for exercise and to have a place to talk. He was also uncomfortable with the situation.

There was another practice session that week in which Shams and I watched the controller who was at the radar console in the administrative building. So far we did nothing ourselves, just observed.

Finally about the 4th week I was allowed to be on the microphone in the tower – it was a minor thrill – the aircraft were cleared for approach and given the current winds and altimeter. The only other vehicles on the airport were maintenance ones and they knew to call the tower and ask permission to transit runways. Nothing exciting there.

With so much time on my hands I would frequently take a handheld radio and go for a walk during the cooler morning hours to enjoy the beauty of the area. There is very little plant life able to sustain itself in the gypsum sands – mostly yucca and a few grasses. There was also a corresponding lack of wildlife and birds on the airport itself.

Just about every day big water trucks would spray down the gypsum runways with water drawn from a manmade pond at the airport's edge. The pond water was extremely alkaline, and the only thing living in it were tiny shrimp.

For a very seldom used airport, WSSH was well maintained.

* * * * *

Stress is Relative!

I was only on my third training session controlling traffic when something interesting occurred. The NASA shuttle was inbound and a vehicle wanted to cross the active runway. Since the aircraft was still more than ten miles out I picked up my walkie-talkie and instructed the van – callsign WSSH2 – to cross the runway. I stayed put.

A minute later he called again requesting to cross the runway. NASA was still a ways out, so I clicked the button on the walkie talkie and said "WSSH2 cleared to cross runway 17 expedite".

Expedite is the term you use to indicate the vehicle is supposed to do something quickly.

The van still did not move and the driver (who was the manager of the airport) again called, with annoyance in his voice, requesting to cross.

By this time it was obvious something was wrong. I wanted to let the vehicle cross and there was still time if it moved quickly. I realized that one of two things might be happening:

- The walkie talkie I held may not be functioning
- The driver of the van might not understand "expedite:"

Trying to address both options I reached over and grabbed my trainer's walkie-talkie and stated "WSHH2 cleared to cross runway 17 – GO FAST!"

Ok, so "Go Fast" is not in any of the ATC manuals, but in cases where you are not sure if the person you are talking to you understands what you want, the manual does allow a controller to use "plain language".

The van crossed the runway without incident and the session continued. My trainer sat through this entire thing without any interference or any suggestions.

It turned out that the walkie talkie I held was dead…but putting it back on the same charger I took it off of that morning livened it up again. Which begs the question, why had it been out of power?

Stress is Relative!

My trainer never said anything, but the airport manager complained about my use of plain language and the delay in his crossing the runway to my boss out in California.

* * * * *

I was only there for a few months when Lockheed's Tower contract was suddenly terminated by the company running the airport. They had determined that with so few shuttle practices being done they did not need to pay another company to manage the tower for them. The two other controllers were kept on by the managing company, but Shams and I were laid off.

So why was the contract allowed to die now? Was it the "official" reason…that there were so few flights more than two controllers were deemed unnecessary? Or was it because Shams and I did not fit the profile of every other employee on the entire airport – white all-american males who probably did not practice a religion outside christianity?

Lockheed Martin had a stated and visibly enforced policy supporting equal employment – hiring Shams and I was a normal step for them. The company that contracted Lockheed to man the Control Tower was less open minded.

In any case, our boss from California came out to meet with us all just before this happened for the first time. He called as I was driving back after a weekend at home in Albuquerque to say both Shams and I were to go back in the morning and be out-processed and pick up our tings. He was very apologetic for the early termination. We were given extra severance pay and he said he'd support any job applications we made to other Lockheed facilities.

I was not going to jump on just anything, I was back in the southwest and planned to stay here. So for a few months I was on unemployment and keeping an eye out for a suitable position.

* * * * *

Stress is Relative!

One night I had a dream. I was in a large building with high ceilings and bright lighting. It was like a large warehouse with racks of clothes, electronic equipment, shelves full of brightly colored fabrics, baskets, rows of flowers and furniture. I wandered up and down hallways and staircases and eventually ended up near the front door.

Outside the sky was darkening and in the distance a tornado formed. It grew larger and larger and I realized it was coming straight at my building. It felt like the building was a manifestation of all the things I had been or could be and its contents were the experiences I'd stored. The tornado coming at me was representing how the loss of my job was threatening both my physical resources and my self-esteem.

I stood transfixed in the doorway, helpless as this dark monster from my childhood nightmares churned towards me.

Suddenly there was a green light just left of the walkway outside of the door which lengthened into a doorway. A man stepped out. It was an old friend from my days back in DC. He looked at the tornado, then he turned to me and said, "Don't worry, it'll be OK." Then he stepped back through the doorway and it disappeared.

At that moment the tornado dissipated into a white whirling cloud and its remnants floated off into a bright blue sky.

I awoke in a happy and peaceful state.

* * * * *

Stress is Relative!

Photo by Jeff Shepard

Prescott AFSS (PRC)

CHAPTER 39

The Prescott Hub

During the time after being laid off from the White Sands job I continued to live with my youngest daughter, Melissa in the Albuquerque home where she'd been housesitting for us since we went to D.C.

My husband was able to affect a transfer to the Prescott Hub and shared a house there with a couple friends. He'd bop home to Albuquerque on weekends, about a six hour drive.

One day I received a call from a friend back in DC who told me that Lockheed had a bid coming out for a Quality Assurance Engineer at the Prescott Hub. (The same one who had invaded my dream!) I think I had my application in 10 seconds after it was posted online.

Getting the job was not a slam dunk. Yes, I had lots of experience and a background in QA, but Lockheed Corporate has a very explicit hiring process. Those candidates with the credentials to get by the initial screening by Human Resources have to have a phone interview which is done by three people who have about 10 questions – none of which has to do with your qualifications.

They figure that background employment information is on the application. What they want to know is what kind of person you are.

Stress is Relative!

The questions are directed at determining how you tend to handle problems, challenges, and relationships. The interviewers want you to answer them in what is referred to as the STAR format.

Situation, Task, Actions, Results (STAR). There is no such thing as a yes or no answer.

The interviewers rate your answers on a 1-10 scale. After everyone is interviewed they pull the top three candidates and discuss them – finally offering the job to whoever they feel would be the best fit.

Luckily, this time it was me. ☺

* * * * *

If I had to end my air traffic career anywhere in the entire country, I could not do better than the Prescott AFSS Hub, and especially with this Quality Assurance Team.

There were six QA's besides me, plus two Plans and Procedures specialists in our office. At one point it was decided to merge the training department with QA – which makes sense really. The QA's all have to be experts in their areas so they are normally working hand in glove with the guys designing the training modules

Our boss, Keith Gosik, had a way of choosing people for the QA staff which centered on specific ideals – people with a history of performance excellence who had a knack for analysis and could smoothly integrate their talents and personalities together. All of us were experts in our areas and all of us backed each other up, so that if someone was out on vacation there was always another qualified to step in.

We were an interesting mix of age and backgrounds. Many, like myself, had been in other air traffic facilities prior to flight service and all branches of the military were represented in the group. When I first arrived all of us had been former FAA employees who'd migrated to Lockheed Martin.

Stress is Relative!

My teammates at Prescott AFSS are what have kept me sane the last few years. Their personalities are quirky but comfortably predictable.

The large QA office is separated with high cubicle walls and my desk is right between John – who plays classical music from the time he enters the building to the time he leaves everyday – and Steve, whose musical taste is more eclectic.

Every now and then I had to stand up and say "ENOUGH!" Have you ever had Rachmaninoff coming from one side and Jethro Tull hitting you from the other?

In most companies, QA is looked at by the employees as "the enemy" because the job involves finding where people are screwing up and reporting them. In this facility, the QA mission is to support operations.

This team doesn't hide in an office and send anonymous reports. We spent a lot of time in operations, sometimes doing the job alongside the specialists on duty in order to keep current on the continuous changes in equipment, weather, and procedures.

If we discovered someone was not performing the job adequately during our evaluations the assumption was that the person is not TRYING to screw up…therefore what they needed was some mentoring. Their supervisor would go over the results of the evaluation and have them go over the pertinent documents. Then the specialist would come to our office for some skill enhancement training.

We always saw it as trying to improve the specialist's work. Most of them were quite cooperative. Now and then you'd get a more difficult personality who was certain that we were just "out to get him". The evaluations were all done randomly and we never knew who was being monitored until the data was plunked down on the desk. Trying to explain that to someone who is not receptive took tact and patience.

That was where this QA team excelled.

In my opinion, the best of us at this was Steve. A former marine, Steve let the difficult specialist rant and rave for about 15 minutes, then he'd pose a question that was just off topic enough to dislodge the bit from

Stress is Relative!

the person's teeth. His quiet voice forced the person to pull back their tirade and his quirky sense of humor cajoled them into looking at the situation reasonably.

Our success rate at helping the specialists improve their performance was well into the 90% range, and over time they grew comfortable with coming to our office and talking to the QAs whenever they were confused about how to apply a new procedure or had questions about the job.

A bittersweet consequence of our success was losing teammates to promotions. Our boss, Keith Gosik (aka YODA) moved into being deputy chief of the facility. My mentor and friend, Kimberly Lindsey, moved into his job, then six months later was asked to take over the QA department in another facility. The next QA chief, Robert, received a lucrative job offer from a rival company. Luckily his replacement, Dustin, was happy being right there in Prescott.

The core group of experienced QAs – me, Steve, John, Mike and Mark, were all content to remain in Prescott until we retired. New blood came in from Operations. Younger and more advanced in computer technology, the two Erics, Tres and Joe brought their knowledge of computer programs and social media into the mix and a dynamic energy that is needed to maintain an edge in this job

Once Kim went to her new job I was the only girl in the office…again. But in this environment I felt respected and wanted from the day I walked in to the day I retired.

* * * * *.

The differences in attitude between working in DCA and PRC were miles apart. Out west there is no less interest in doing the job correctly and efficiently, but the attitudes are mellower overall.

Stress is Relative!

The Operations Room

Most of the specialists in Operations could come to work in blue jeans and clean t-shirts. In the QA department we customarily wore business casual. I am telling you right now business casual in Arizona is WAY more relaxed than business casual in Virginia!

I became a "Subject Matter Expert" (SME) in a couple areas, one of which (NOTAMs) underwent massive changes over a four year period to the point that I made sure every specialist had my office phone number so they could call me if something came up they needed help with.

Some days I would walk into the office where the call light on my phone was flashing and as I was dialing for messages I had the facility manager at my door and emails coming up on the computer all dealing with NOTAM problems.

During this time all the NOTAM SME's across the nation were actively engaged with the FAA in working out analytical tools for performance management. Some of us also helped the U.S. NOTAM office with proofreading their revised handbook. The third national award I received was as part of this dynamite team.

. . * * * * *

Stress is Relative!

One of the extra functions I did, both with the FAA and Lockheed Martin, was to represent them to various aviation groups. I gave presentations to pilots at flying events and to airport managers on topics related to Flight Service.

I became an aviation history buff and was asked by Embry Riddle University to give a presentation on the history of Air Traffic Control at their monthly Aviation History program. The 300 seat auditorium at the Prescott Campus was full.

Rose lecturing at Embry Riddle University

* * * * *

In 2017 I was asked to give the program again at the Museum of Aviation History in Oshkosh, Wisconsin during AirVenture. The Experimental Aircraft Association's AirVenture is the largest aviation event in the world. For one week in late summer over 100,000 aircraft and half a million people travel to this small town to celebrate the joy of aviation.

Stress is Relative!

Vintage aircraft, warbirds, corporate jets, helicopters, drones, gliders and just about anything else that flies can be found there. The sound of jets and bi-planes doing aerobatics dominates the airfield. Hundreds fly in and camp under the wings of their aircraft!

The North 40 at Oshkosh during the EAA's AirVenture – where pilots camp out next to their aircraft.

Stress is Relative!

During AirVenture Rose lectured at the Museum of Aviation History and did book signing at shops throughout the airfield.

Stress is Relative!

CHAPTER 40

A Dirty Little Secret about Stress

Throughout my life whenever I tell people I work in Air Traffic Control, 95% of them immediately make a comment about it being a stressful job.

This is one of the best pieces of propaganda ever used on the American public by a union.

From what you've read so far you will have noticed that there are times when the job is stressful and there are times it is not. Not every Air Traffic Control facility runs the same amount and diversity of aircraft. There are ATC Towers at many airports which serve relatively low levels of traffic.

The sheer number of aircraft in Chicago, Atlanta, and the other large cities ensure the controllers must be at the top of their game every time they are on duty. To mitigate the challenge, these airports only serve jet aircraft. Aircraft inbound to these airports are sequenced and lined up hundreds of miles away so the tower only has to make sure the pilots do not deviate from the plan.

Other airports serve fewer aircraft, but the diversity of aircraft creates a greater complexity factor. Albuquerque International is one that handles a fair number of air carriers, military jets, helicopters, private jets and small general aviation aircraft.

Stress is Relative!

There are hundreds of airports with towers that have less traffic. In fact, the FAA designates 12 levels of Tower traffic based on numbers and complexity. There are far more level one thru level three towers than there are level 12.

There are over 500 Towers across the nation, nearly 200 are managed by private corporations – these are levels one through three. There are only about ten Level 12 towers and an equal number of Level 11 towers.

Each facility, ARTCC, Tower or Flight Service has periods of the day when traffic is high and other times when the controllers are sitting around waiting for something to happen.

Some people who work in Air Traffic choose to work facilities with higher levels of traffic because the paycheck is higher and they like the adrenaline rush. Other people enjoy a career at a lower level facility that still pays fairly well but has fewer aircraft.

When I look at police, firemen, soldiers, and others like them I see people whose jobs are a lot more stressful and yet they don't get paid nearly as well and they are outside in all kinds of weather.

Garbage men, electric company linemen, people working construction, farm hands…all these people have to work in the heat, cold, rain and snow and don't make nearly as much money as controllers. But all these people have families and bills to pay.

Controllers work in climate controlled facilities with comfortable chairs and frequent breaks. They don't have to face down criminals, their own lives are not threatened on duty.

They do not require college degrees to do the job, the FAA trains them while under salary. They must have the ability to memorize, interpret data and make quick decisions based on current situations. When they go home at the end of the day there is nothing left undone. Once they pass the position to the next controller they are finished and can go home without worrying that some task did not get accomplished.

I know some controllers who love their jobs, I know others who hate it, but love the money.

Stress is Relative!

Yes, everyone who works in this industry must keep in mind that the instructions they issue to pilots affect all the people in an aircraft and never become complacent. But when I look at the big picture of this job which commands respect and pays really well versus the others mentioned above…well, like I said…Stress is Relative.

Stress is Relative!

Briefing pilots at Prescott Flight Service

Stress is Relative!

CHAPTER 41

All Good Things End

In April, 2017 I retired from my job as a QA Engineer for Flight Service. The past 34 years since I entered this job has seen dramatic changes in the diversity of people working in ATC. Women now pursue widely varied careers including that of pilots and controllers, without getting automatically sneered at. Are things perfect? No.

Ideals are good – they give the population as a whole a direction to travel. Individuals choose whether to embrace those ideals or travel through life as schmucks. The schmucks are mostly held in check only because there are laws which tell them to behave or be punished.

I am old enough now to tell the schmucks to kiss off. I can look back over my career and know that I succeeded in becoming one of the best despite their actions.

* * * * *

There have been many truly gifted and generous men and women who have guided me and encouraged me. My supervisors at Albuquerque, especially Dennis Livesay and Thom Ochello did everything in their power to ensure I was recognized for my abilities.

My QA managers Scott Cunningham, Glenn Reffner, Keith Gosik and Kimberley Lindsey gave me new avenues to pursue with challenges I enjoy.

Stress is Relative!

Retiring now is appropriate. Flight Service as an entity is slowly dissolving. Many of the functions it was created to provide are now more effectively served through today's advanced technology. Flight Service was the first arm of Air Traffic Control. Over time its functions changed, but its mission – to serve the pilot's needs – has not.

The Towers and Centers are being equipped with technology that makes doing the job easier and may eventually reduce the need for human intervention. Someday the planes will fly themselves with pilots on board only in case of equipment malfunction.

The duties of Flight Service are being spun off slowly as well. Many general aviation pilots file their flight plans and research preflight briefing information and weather themselves now rather than call Flight Service. The advent of satellite based aircraft tracking will significantly reduce the need for our present Search and Rescue responsibilities – ATC will immediately know where an aircraft goes down rather than having to spend time searching for it.

Other aspects of the job are being automated to the point that they only require a little oversite. Although the Towers and Centers are still hiring and trying to build up their workforce, Flight Service has been allowing theirs to attrite slowly.

It has been 36 years since the Air Traffic Control strike, and the huge workforce created in its wake is aging. All of them were eligible to retire years ago though some stayed in staff positions. A new generation of controllers is being trained, and the percentage of female controllers is slowly rising.

I am still working with aviation groups and am a member of several including *Women in Aviation, AOPA* and the *Experimental Aircraft Association*.

Stress is Relative!

I have enjoyed working in aviation, and plan to do some research for a book on ATC history. As a volunteer I am certified as an FAA Safety Team member, able to give presentations on aviation weather and current safety tips to pilot groups.

During the past 34 years I have watched women become accepted as competent in a challenging profession and though the percentage overall is still small, that is more attributable to the lack of information at a young age than of societal prejudice. I'd still like to see some pilot Barbie dolls, or some other way of introducing women to the delights of flight early in life.

Thank you to the FAA for giving me a chance to prove myself, and provide a good life for my daughters. Thank you to Lockheed Martin for bringing new challenges and rewards my way.

Mostly, thank you Mom and Dad, for teaching us responsibility and integrity and never telling your daughters we couldn't do something because we were girls.

OVER AND OUT

Stress is Relative!

If you would like to meet Rose Marie and attend one of her presentations, check out her schedule on www.rosemariekern.com.

Stress is Relative!

Air to Ground

by

Rose Marie Kern

An Air Traffic Control specialist for over 34 years, first with the Federal Government and later with Lockheed Martin, Rose Marie Kern has written articles for 17 different aviation magazines and newsletters and is a popular speaker for pilot associations. *Air to Ground*, gives pilots a glimpse into the cold corridors of Air Traffic, and allows them insights into the people who work in an environment so critical to their own.

Air to Ground contains current and historical data on the National Airspace System, the Air Traffic Control System, and aviation weather in a way that is friendly, easily readable and understandable to even the most novice pilot. It is not meant to replace the government's directives, but to supplement them.

Although there are a few books that talk about Air Traffic on the market, no other book approaches the pilot from this perspective, it fills a vacancy long overlooked. Intermingled with the technical information are stories and snippets of humor collected over the last 33 years. These little bits exemplify what happens in the Air Traffic workplace when the microphone is not keyed, humanizing the disembodied voices the pilots hear.

"Air to Ground" is a phrase used to describe the frequencies used by the pilots when they speak to Air Traffic.

The book, *Air to Ground*, appeals to pilots, airport managers and the air traffic personnel who work in the U.S. and will greatly enhance the pilot's understanding of the National Airspace System, its procedures, and the people whose job it is to provide for the safe and efficient flow of Air Traffic.

Available on Amazon or through www.rosemariekern.com

Stress is Relative!

Vengeance Ends at Oshkosh

An Upcoming Book by Rose Marie Kern

Rose Marie Kern dives into fiction novel writing for the first time with a murder/mystery based in the wide world of aviation.

Vengeance at Oshkosh follows NTSB inspector Lindsey Mitchell as she investigates what seems to be a series of unrelated aircraft accidents, except that all of the pilots served together thirty years earlier in the Air Force during the Vietnam conflict.

When she discovers that her husband also flew with the same squadron the need to find out what is happening intensifies.

Vengeance at Oshkosh is due to be released in April of 2109. Monitor Rose Marie's website for details. www.rosemariekern.com

www.ingramcontent.com/pod-product-compliance
Lightning Source LLC
Chambersburg PA
CBHW070421010526
44118CB00014B/1853